Report To The Commission To Assess United States National Security Space Management And Organization

Donald F. Rumsfeld

NIMBLE BOOKS LLC: THE AI LAB FOR BOOK-LOVERS

~ FRED ZIMMERMAN, EDITOR ~

Humans and AI making books richer, more diverse, and more surprising.

Publishing Information

(c) 2024 Nimble Books LLC
ISBN: 978-1-60888-312-7

AI-generated Keyword Phrases

Defense in space; Satellite Operations; Satellite Services; A New Military Department for Space; Under Secretary of Defense for Space, Intelligence and Information; Space Intelligence Security and Information Operations; Space systems management; Under Secretary of the Air Force SecAF; Secretary of the Army SecArmy; Secretary of the Army SecDef; Secretary of Defense SecNav; Secretary of Navy.

Publisher's Notes

America's future security and prosperity are inextricably linked to our ability to operate freely in space. From the mundane, such as using your cell phone, to the critical, such as gathering intelligence on terrorist threats, American life and American security depend upon space-based assets. But these assets are vulnerable. This book details how the United States can best organize itself to protect its space-based interests, which are essential to our economy, our national security, and our way of life.

This annotated edition illustrates the capabilities of the AI Lab for Book-Lovers to add context and ease-of-use to manuscripts. It includes several types of abstracts, building from simplest to more complex: TLDR (one word), ELI5, TLDR (vanilla), Scientific Style, and Action Items; essays to increase viewpoint diversity, such as Grounds for Dissent, Red Team Critique, and MAGA Perspective; and Notable Passages and Nutshell Summaries for each page.

ANNOTATIONS

Publishing Information ii
AI-generated Keyword Phrases ii
Publisher's Notes ii
Abstracts iv
    TL;DR (one word) iv
    Explain It To Me Like I'm Five Years Old iv
    TL;DR (vanilla) iv
    Simple Summary iv
    Action Items v
    Scientific Style v
Viewpoints vi
    Rumsfeld Snowflakes vi
Space: The 2000 Report's "Unknown Unknowns" -
    A Snowflake Memo for 2024 vi
The 2000 Report - A Cry in the Wilderness vii
The Unknown Unknowns: Are We Prepared? ... vii
What Should We Take Away? vii
    Red Team Critique viii
    MAGA Perspective ix
Seven Striking Passages x

Abstracts

TL;DR (one word)

Spacedefense.[1]

Explain It To Me Like I'm Five Years Old

Defense in space means keeping our satellites and other space activities safe from any threats. This is important because satellites help us with things like communication, GPS, and observing our planet.

Satellite operations are the ways we control and use satellites in space. We need to make sure they work properly and do what we need them to do.

Satellite services are the things we use satellites for, like communication, weather monitoring, and navigation.

A new military department for space would be a special group of people.

TL;DR (vanilla)

The Department of Defense is considering creating a new military department for space operations, with an Under Secretary of Defense for Space, Intelligence and Information. This new department would oversee satellite operations, services, and security in space.

Simple Summary

Defense in space has become a growing concern as satellite operations and services become increasingly vital to national security. A new military department for space has been established, with the Under Secretary of Defense for Space, Intelligence and Information overseeing space intelligence security and information operations. Current management of space activity at the national level, within the Department of Defense and Intelligence Community, highlights the importance of effective space systems management in maintaining security and stability in the ever-evolving space domain.

---

[1] The AI came up with this innovation on its own. —Ed.

ACTION ITEMS

Establish a new military department specifically dedicated to space operations, with a focus on defense and intelligence gathering.

Appoint an Under Secretary of Defense for Space, Intelligence, and Information to oversee and coordinate space activities within the Department of Defense and the Intelligence Community.

Enhance satellite operations and services to improve communication, surveillance, and reconnaissance capabilities in space.

Develop and implement a comprehensive strategy for defending U.S. interests in space, including identifying and mitigating potential threats from other countries or non-state actors.

Increase collaboration and coordination between the military branches, intelligence agencies, and private sector partners involved in

SCIENTIFIC STYLE

This report, prepared for the U.S. Congress, assesses the management and organization of the national security space activities of the United States Government. The report identifies U.S. national interests in space and measures that can be undertaken to advance them.

The report provides a summary of the organizations involved in space activities, focusing on the Executive Office of the President, the Department of Defense, the Intelligence Community, and the U.S. Congress. The report analyzes the management of national security space activities from the standpoints of interagency coordination, the relationship between the Secretary of Defense and the Director of Central Intelligence, processes for acquiring and operating space systems, the pursuit of "leap ahead" technologies, leveraging commercial and civil capabilities, methods of budgeting for space programs, and the use of space capabilities in exercises, experiments and wargames.

The report concludes with a set of recommendations to improve the management and organization of national security space activities in the United States Government, concentrating on recommendations directed to the President; to the Secretary of Defense and the Director of Central Intelligence; to the Department of the Air Force and the National Reconnaissance Office; and to the U.S. Congress.

VIEWPOINTS

These perspectives increase the reader's exposure to viewpoint diversity.

RUMSFELD SNOWFLAKES

Donald Rumsfeld was known for his distinctive "snowflake" memos - short, often blunt, and always focused on driving action. These memos were notorious for their unconventional format, frequently including pointed questions and thought-provoking challenges. They were not meant to be exhaustive reports or detailed policy analyses, but rather catalysts for debate, forcing recipients to confront issues head-on and engage in creative problem-solving. Rumsfeld believed in using these memos to cut through bureaucracy, challenge assumptions, and inspire fresh thinking.

Here's a breakdown of his key techniques:

__1. The "Unknown Unknowns" Challenge:__ Rumsfeld famously used the phrase "unknown unknowns" to highlight the need to acknowledge and address unanticipated challenges. His memos often prompted recipients to think about potential threats they hadn't yet considered, forcing them to be more proactive and less reactive.

__2. Provocative Questions:__ Rumsfeld's memos often featured pointed questions that forced recipients to re-examine their assumptions and consider alternative perspectives. These questions were not meant to be rhetorical, but rather to spark real dialogue and generate new ideas.

__3. Direct and Concise:__ Rumsfeld's memos were short and to the point, avoiding unnecessary jargon and convoluted language. He believed in getting to the heart of the issue quickly and efficiently, and encouraged others to do the same.

__4. Action-Oriented:__ The primary goal of Rumsfeld's memos was to drive action. They often concluded with specific directives or tasks, demanding a concrete and immediate response from recipients. He was fond of Churchill's phrase "Action This Day."

__5. A "Snowflake" Format:__ Rumsfeld's memos were often unconventional in their format, using boldface type, bullet points, and other visual elements to emphasize key points and create a memorable impact. This unorthodox approach helped cut through the noise and ensure the memo's message was received clearly.

I asked the model to apply Rumsfeld's snowflake methods to provide the 2024 reader with perspective on the 2000 report. —Ed.

SPACE: THE 2000 REPORT'S "UNKNOWN UNKNOWNS" - A SNOWFLAKE MEMO FOR 2024

To: Anyone Concerned with the Future of Space

From: The Ghosts of Space Policy Past

Subject: 2000: The Year We Got the Warning, but Didn't Really Notice

Challenge: Fast forward to 2024. We're in a different world than 2000. Space is now a major geopolitical stage, not just a scientific frontier. But are we prepared for the "unknown unknowns" we didn't even imagine back then?

THE 2000 REPORT - A CRY IN THE WILDERNESS

- **Space is no longer a "luxury"**: That report, penned by a committee chaired by a certain Donald Rumsfeld, sounded the alarm about our growing dependence on space - and the vulnerabilities that came with it. We were already reliant on satellites for comms, navigation, intelligence, and even weather forecasting. But we weren't taking the threat seriously enough.
- **It's not just other nations we need to worry about**: Back then, the report warned about the potential for "Space Pearl Harbor" attacks by hostile states, but technology has democratized space. We're now dealing with non-state actors, proliferating technology, and a world where even a small nation can disrupt our critical systems.
- **The "interagency" process was a mess then, and it's still a mess now**: The report called out the lack of unified leadership and coordination across government agencies. We're still struggling with this, and it's costing us dearly in terms of wasted resources and lost opportunities.
- **The Air Force was in denial then, and they're still struggling to catch up**: They were slow to embrace space as a core mission, focusing on air power instead. That attitude has hampered our overall space strategy.

THE UNKNOWN UNKNOWNS: ARE WE PREPARED?

- **Space as a battlefield:** That 2000 report was prescient in its warnings about the militarization of space. We're seeing it happen now, with space becoming a critical piece of the modern battlefield, from ISR (intelligence, surveillance, and reconnaissance) to space-based weapons systems.
- **Cyberwar in space:** The report didn't anticipate cyberwarfare, but it's become a major threat, targeting ground stations and disrupting satellites.
- **The rise of space debris:** The report flagged the danger of collisions with space debris, a problem that's only getting worse. We're facing a potential "Kessler Syndrome" where the Earth is engulfed by a cloud of debris, making space unusable.

WHAT SHOULD WE TAKE AWAY?

- **Space is critical to our national security**: We can't afford to be caught flat-footed. We need to prioritize space capabilities, invest in technological innovation, and build a more resilient space infrastructure.

- **The 2000 report wasn't just a warning, it was a roadmap**: We need to get serious about the recommendations in that report - unified leadership, a more integrated approach to space management, and a dedicated focus on space capabilities.
- **The unknown unknowns are coming:** We need to be prepared to adapt and innovate, and invest in the people, technologies, and organizations that will ensure the future of our nation in space.

Action: This memo is a wake-up call, not a policy analysis. It's time to get to work, or risk losing the space race altogether. The future of our nation depends on it.

RED TEAM CRITIQUE

Retrospective.

The document "Defense in Space" provides a high-level overview of satellite operations and services, as well as the proposal for a new military department for space. However, there are several key areas that need further clarification and development.

Firstly, the document lacks a comprehensive analysis of the current threats and challenges facing space operations. It briefly mentions the need for defense in space, but fails to provide specific information on potential adversaries, their capabilities, and the risks they pose to satellite operations. This oversight limits the effectiveness of the proposed solutions and strategies outlined in the document.

Secondly, the organizational structure proposed for the new military department for space is vague and lacks detail. The document mentions the creation of an Under Secretary of Defense for Space, Intelligence, and Information, but does not clearly define the roles and responsibilities of this new position or how it will interact with existing military departments and agencies. Without a clear understanding of how this new department will be structured and integrated into the larger national security framework, it is difficult to assess the feasibility and effectiveness of the proposed changes.

Additionally, the document does not address the potential budgetary implications of establishing a new military department for space. It is important to consider the cost of creating and maintaining this new organization, as well as the potential trade-offs with other defense priorities. Without a thorough cost-benefit analysis, it is difficult to assess the long-term sustainability and impact of the proposed changes.

Overall, while the document provides a basic overview of the need for defense in space and the proposal for a new military department, it lacks the depth and specificity required to effectively address the complex and evolving challenges of space operations. A more detailed analysis of threats, organizational structure, and budget considerations is necessary to ensure the success of any proposed changes in this critical domain.

MAGA Perspective

Retrospective: if we had MAGA in 2001!

This document is just another example of the deep state pushing for increased government control and spending in the name of "defense in space." The idea of creating a new military department for space is a waste of taxpayer dollars and a power grab by those in positions of authority. We already have an Air Force and other branches of the military that can handle any potential threats in space.

The notion of a Under Secretary of Defense for Space, Intelligence, and Information is just a way to further expand the bureaucratic mess that already exists within the government. This is nothing more than a way for politicians and bureaucrats to consolidate power and control over space operations without any real benefit to the American people. This is just another example of government overreach and waste.

The current management of space activity at the national level is already efficient and effective, there is no need to create a new department just to satisfy the egos of those in power. This document is nothing more than a political stunt to try to score points with the defense industry and lobbyists who stand to benefit from increased spending on space operations. The American people do not want or need this kind of bloated bureaucracy.

Satellite operations and services can be handled within the existing structures of the military and intelligence community, there is no need for a whole new department to be created. The push for this new department is just a way for those in power to increase their influence and control over critical national security operations. This document is nothing more than a power grab disguised as a necessary security measure.

In conclusion, the creation of a new military department for space is unnecessary and a waste of taxpayer dollars. The current system is already working efficiently and effectively, there is no need to add another layer of bureaucracy to an already bloated government. This document is just another example of the swamp trying to expand its power and control at the expense of the American people.

Seven Striking Passages

Here are seven passages from the 2000 report that stand out for a reader in 2024, highlighting the report's prescience and relevance to today's space landscape.

"The security and economic well being of the United States and its allies and friends depend on the nation's ability to operate successfully in space." (Page 9)

This statement, though commonplace today, was a bold proclamation in 2000. It foreshadows the widespread dependence on space for communication, navigation, and other critical services that we now take for granted.

"Space is not simply a place from which information is acquired and transmitted or through which objects pass. It is a medium much the same as air, land or sea." (Page 13)

This passage captures the report's understanding of space as a strategic domain, not just a passive environment. This perspective resonates deeply with the militarization of space that we're seeing in 2024.

"The U.S. is an attractive candidate for a "Space Pearl Harbor." (Page 22)

This stark warning, though perhaps hyperbolic in 2000, has become more relevant in light of the increasing vulnerability of space assets and the rise of new threats. It underscores the need for proactive defense strategies in space.

"The ability to restrict or deny freedom of access to and operations in space is no longer limited to global military powers. Knowledge of space systems and the means to counter them is increasingly available on the international market." (Page 19)

This passage prophetically highlights the democratization of space technology, a trend that has significantly altered the space security landscape. It anticipates the growing threat posed by non-state actors and smaller nations.

"The Intelligence Community needs to get its act together and stop playing catch-up. We need revolutionary collection methods, not just incremental improvements, and we need to know what our adversaries are thinking, not just what they're doing." (Page 98)

The report's call for a more proactive and insightful intelligence approach resonates deeply with the ongoing challenges of understanding the motivations and capabilities of adversaries in space, especially in the context of cyberwarfare.

"Space capabilities are not funded at a level commensurate with their relative importance. Nor is there a plan in place to build up to the investments needed to modernize existing systems and procure new capabilities." (Page 97)

The report's lament about underfunding of space programs is unfortunately still relevant today. It underscores the ongoing struggle to secure adequate resources for space security initiatives.

"The unknown unknowns are coming: We need to be prepared to adapt and innovate, and invest in the people, technologies, and organizations that will ensure the future of our nation in space." (Page 102)

This concluding call to action encapsulates the report's primary message: the need for foresight, adaptability, and investment in order to secure the future of the United States as a leading space power. This remains a crucial message for decision-makers in 2024.

These passages demonstrate the prescience of the 2000 report. The issues it addressed – the growing dependence on space, the evolving threat landscape, and the need for proactive space management – continue to be critical concerns for policymakers and citizens alike. The report serves as a reminder that vigilance, innovation, and robust investment are essential for maintaining U.S. dominance in the space domain.

Report of the

COMMISSION TO ASSESS UNITED STATES NATIONAL SECURITY SPACE MANAGEMENT AND ORGANIZATION

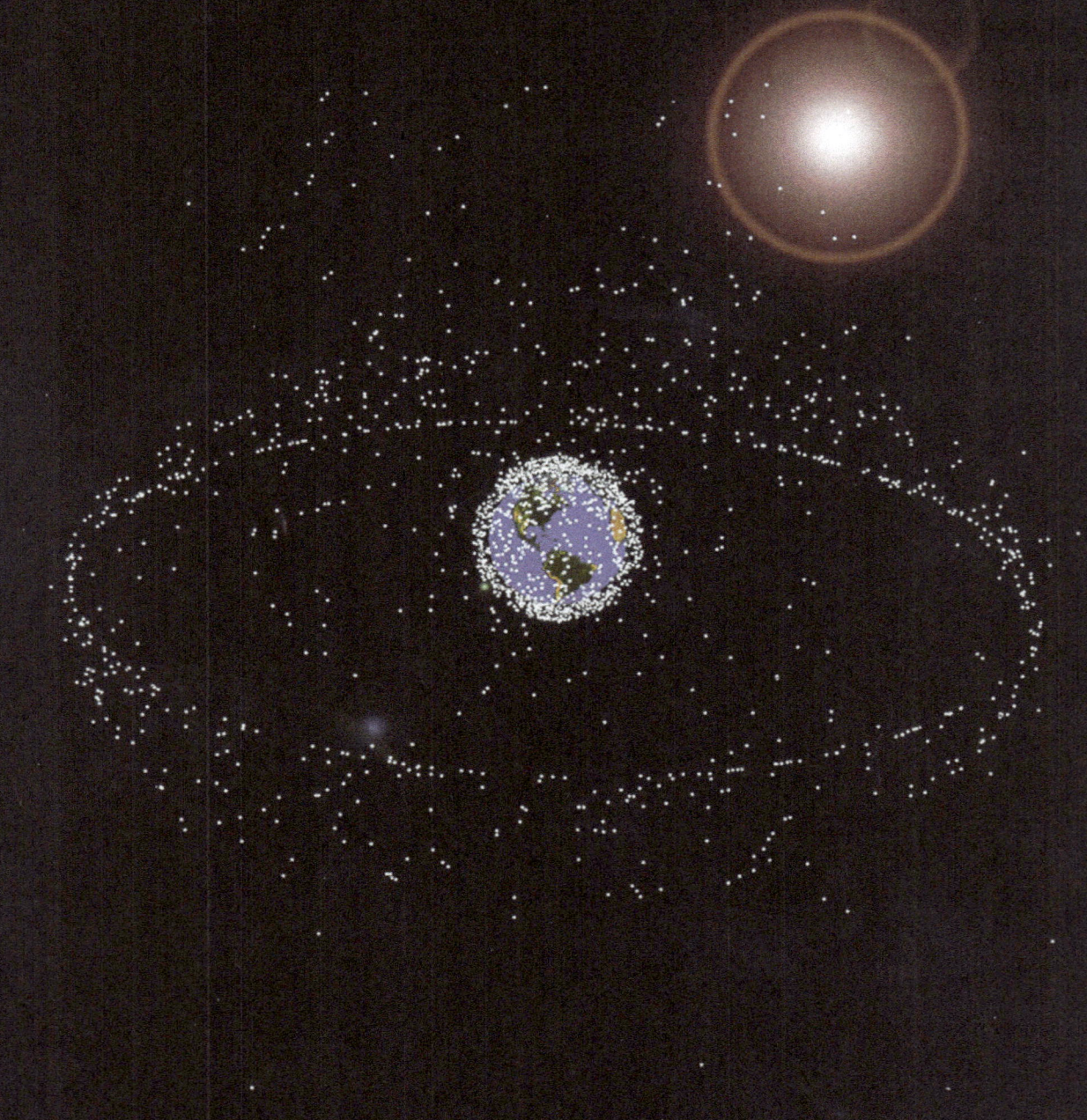

Pursuant to Public Law 106-65
January 11, 2001

Report Documentation Page

Report Date 11 Jan 2001	Report Type N/A	Dates Covered (from... to) -

Title and Subtitle Report to the Commission to Assess United States National Security Space Management and Organization	Contract Number
	Grant Number
	Program Element Number
Author(s)	Project Number
	Task Number
	Work Unit Number
Performing Organization Name(s) and Address(es) Commission to Assess United States National Security Space Management and Organization Washington D C 20033-0633	Performing Organization Report Number
Sponsoring/Monitoring Agency Name(s) and Address(es)	Sponsor/Monitor's Acronym(s)
	Sponsor/Monitor's Report Number(s)

Distribution/Availability Statement
Approved for public release, distribution unlimited

Supplementary Notes
The original document contains color images.

Abstract

Subject Terms

Report Classification unclassified	Classification of this page unclassified
Classification of Abstract unclassified	Limitation of Abstract UU

Number of Pages
164

Report of the

**COMMISSION TO ASSESS
UNITED STATES NATIONAL SECURITY SPACE
MANAGEMENT AND ORGANIZATION**

Pursuant to Public Law 106-65
January 11, 2001

Commission to Assess United States National Security Space Management and Organization

PO BOX 33633
WASHINGTON DC 20033-0633

Hon. Donald H. Rumsfeld *
Chairman

Hon. Duane P. Andrews
Mr. Robert V. Davis
Gen. Howell M. Estes, III, USAF (Ret.)
Gen. Ronald R. Fogleman, USAF (Ret.)
LTG Jay M. Garner, USA (Ret.)
Hon. William R. Graham

Gen. Charles A. Horner, USAF (Ret.)
ADM David E. Jeremiah, USN (Ret.)
Gen. Thomas S. Moorman, Jr., USAF (Ret.)
Mr. Douglas H. Necessary
GEN Glenn K. Otis, USA (Ret.)
Sen. Malcolm Wallop (ret.)

January 11, 2001

Chairman
Committee on Armed Services of the U.S. House of Representatives
Washington, DC 20515-6035

Dear Mr. Chairman:

In accordance with section 1623 of the National Defense Authorization Act for Fiscal Year 2000 (P.L. 106-65), we hereby submit the report of the Commission to Assess United States National Security Space Management and Organization. The Commission's report is unanimous. It has been an honor to serve.

Respectfully submitted,

Duane P. Andrews
Robert V. Davis
Howell M. Estes, III
Ronald R. Fogleman
Jay M. Garner
William R. Graham
Charles A. Horner
David E. Jeremiah
Thomas S. Moorman, Jr.
Douglas H. Necessary
Glenn K. Otis
Malcolm Wallop

---

* The Honorable Donald H. Rumsfeld served as a member and chairman of the Commission from its inception until December 28, 2000, when he was nominated for the position of Secretary of Defense by President-elect George W. Bush.

Commission to Assess United States National Security Space Management and Organization

PO BOX 33633
WASHINGTON DC 20033-0633

Hon. Donald H. Rumsfeld *
Chairman

Hon. Duane P. Andrews
Mr. Robert V. Davis
Gen. Howell M. Estes, III, USAF (Ret.)
Gen. Ronald R. Fogleman, USAF (Ret.)
LTG Jay M. Garner, USA (Ret.)
Hon. William R. Graham

Gen. Charles A. Horner, USAF (Ret.)
ADM David E. Jeremiah, USN (Ret.)
Gen. Thomas S. Moorman, Jr., USAF (Ret.)
Mr. Douglas H. Necessary
GEN Glenn K. Otis, USA (Ret.)
Sen. Malcolm Wallop (ret.)

January 11, 2001

The Honorable Ike Skelton
Ranking Minority Member
Committee on Armed Services of the U.S. House of Representatives
Washington, DC 20515-6035

Dear Mr. Skelton:

In accordance with section 1623 of the National Defense Authorization Act for Fiscal Year 2000 (P.L. 106-65), we hereby submit the report of the Commission to Assess United States National Security Space Management and Organization. The Commission's report is unanimous. It has been an honor to serve.

Respectfully submitted,

Duane P. Andrews   Robert V. Davis   Howell M. Estes, III

Ronald R. Fogleman   Jay M. Garner   William R. Graham

Charles A. Horner   David E. Jeremiah   Thomas S. Moorman, Jr.

Douglas H. Necessary   Glenn K. Otis   Malcolm Wallop

---

* The Honorable Donald H. Rumsfeld served as a member and chairman of the Commission from its inception until December 28, 2000, when he was nominated for the position of Secretary of Defense by President-elect George W. Bush.

Commission to Assess United States National Security Space Management and Organization

PO BOX 33633
WASHINGTON DC 20033-0633

Hon. Donald H. Rumsfeld *
Chairman

Hon. Duane P. Andrews
Mr. Robert V. Davis
Gen. Howell M. Estes, III, USAF (Ret.)
Gen. Ronald R. Fogleman, USAF (Ret.)
LTG Jay M. Garner, USA (Ret.)
Hon. William R. Graham

Gen. Charles A. Horner, USAF (Ret.)
ADM David E. Jeremiah, USN (Ret.)
Gen. Thomas S. Moorman, Jr., USAF (Ret.)
Mr. Douglas H. Necessary
GEN Glenn K. Otis, USA (Ret.)
Sen. Malcolm Wallop (ret.)

January 11, 2001

The Honorable Carl Levin
Chairman
Committee on Armed Services of the U.S. Senate
Washington, DC 20510-6050

Dear Mr. Chairman:

    In accordance with section 1623 of the National Defense Authorization Act for Fiscal Year 2000 (P.L. 106-65), we hereby submit the report of the Commission to Assess United States National Security Space Management and Organization. The Commission's report is unanimous. It has been an honor to serve.

Respectfully submitted,

Duane P. Andrews   _Robert V. Davis_   _Howell M. Estes, III_

Ronald R. Fogleman   _Jay M. Garner_   _William R. Graham_

Charles A. Horner   _David E. Jeremiah_   _Thomas S. Moorman, Jr._

Douglas H. Necessary   _Glenn K. Otis_   _Malcolm Wallop_

---

* The Honorable Donald H. Rumsfeld served as a member and chairman of the Commission from its inception until December 28, 2000, when he was nominated for the position of Secretary of Defense by President-elect George W. Bush.

Commission to Assess United States National Security Space Management and Organization

PO BOX 33633
WASHINGTON DC 20033-0633

Hon. Donald H. Rumsfeld *
Chairman

Hon. Duane P. Andrews
Mr. Robert V. Davis
Gen. Howell M. Estes, III, USAF (Ret.)
Gen. Ronald R. Fogleman, USAF (Ret.)
LTG Jay M. Garner, USA (Ret.)
Hon. William R. Graham

Gen. Charles A. Horner, USAF (Ret.)
ADM David E. Jeremiah, USN (Ret.)
Gen. Thomas S. Moorman, Jr., USAF (Ret.)
Mr. Douglas H. Necessary
GEN Glenn K. Otis, USA (Ret.)
Sen. Malcolm Wallop (ret.)

January 11, 2001

The Honorable John Warner
Ranking Minority Member
Committee on Armed Services of the U.S. Senate
Washington, DC 20510-6050

Dear Senator Warner:

In accordance with section 1623 of the National Defense Authorization Act for Fiscal Year 2000 (P.L. 106-65), we hereby submit the report of the Commission to Assess United States National Security Space Management and Organization. The Commission's report is unanimous. It has been an honor to serve.

Respectfully submitted,

Duane P. Andrews

Robert V. Davis

Howell M. Estes, III

Ronald R. Fogleman

Jay M. Garner

William R. Graham

Charles A. Horner

David E. Jeremiah

Thomas S. Moorman, Jr.

Douglas H. Necessary

Glenn K. Otis

Malcolm Wallop

---

* The Honorable Donald H. Rumsfeld served as a member and chairman of the Commission from its inception until December 28, 2000, when he was nominated for the position of Secretary of Defense by President-elect George W. Bush.

Commission to Assess United States National Security Space Management and Organization

PO BOX 33633
WASHINGTON DC 20033-0633

Hon. Donald H. Rumsfeld *
Chairman

Hon. Duane P. Andrews	Gen. Charles A. Horner, USAF (Ret.)
Mr. Robert V. Davis	ADM David E. Jeremiah, USN (Ret.)
Gen. Howell M. Estes, III, USAF (Ret.)	Gen. Thomas S. Moorman, Jr., USAF (Ret.)
Gen. Ronald R. Fogleman, USAF (Ret.)	Mr. Douglas H. Necessary
LTG Jay M. Garner, USA (Ret.)	GEN Glenn K. Otis, USA (Ret.)
Hon. William R. Graham	Sen. Malcolm Wallop (ret.)

January 11, 2001

The Honorable J. Dennis Hastert
Speaker of the United States House of Representatives
Washington, DC 20515

Dear Mr. Speaker:

    In accordance with section 1623 of the National Defense Authorization Act for Fiscal Year 2000 (P.L. 106-65), we hereby submit the report of the Commission to Assess United States National Security Space Management and Organization. The Commission's report is unanimous. It has been an honor to serve.

Respectfully submitted,

Duane P. Andrews   _Robert V. Davis_   _Howell M. Estes, III_

Ronald R. Fogleman   _Jay M. Garner_   _William R. Graham_

Charles A. Horner   _David E. Jeremiah_   _Thomas S. Moorman, Jr._

Douglas H. Necessary   _Glenn K. Otis_   _Malcolm Wallop_

---

* The Honorable Donald H. Rumsfeld served as a member and chairman of the Commission from its inception until December 28, 2000, when he was nominated for the position of Secretary of Defense by President-elect George W. Bush.

Commission to Assess United States National Security Space Management and Organization

PO BOX 33633
WASHINGTON DC 20033-0633

Hon. Donald H. Rumsfeld[*]
Chairman

Hon. Duane P. Andrews
Mr. Robert V. Davis
Gen. Howell M. Estes, III, USAF (Ret.)
Gen. Ronald R. Fogleman, USAF (Ret.)
LTG Jay M. Garner, USA (Ret.)
Hon. William R. Graham

Gen. Charles A. Horner, USAF (Ret.)
ADM David E. Jeremiah, USN (Ret.)
Gen. Thomas S. Moorman, Jr., USAF (Ret.)
Mr. Douglas H. Necessary
GEN Glenn K. Otis, USA (Ret.)
Sen. Malcolm Wallop (ret.)

January 11, 2001

The Honorable Richard A. Gephardt
Minority Leader
United States House of Representatives
Washington, DC 20515

Dear Mr. Gephardt:

In accordance with section 1623 of the National Defense Authorization Act for Fiscal Year 2000 (P.L. 106-65), we hereby submit the report of the Commission to Assess United States National Security Space Management and Organization. The Commission's report is unanimous. It has been an honor to serve.

Respectfully submitted,

Duane P. Andrews

Robert V. Davis

Howell M. Estes, III

Ronald R. Fogleman

Jay M. Garner

William R. Graham

Charles A. Horner

David E. Jeremiah

Thomas S. Moorman, Jr.

Douglas H. Necessary

Glenn K. Otis

Malcolm Wallop

---

[*] The Honorable Donald H. Rumsfeld served as a member and chairman of the Commission from its inception until December 28, 2000, when he was nominated for the position of Secretary of Defense by President-elect George W. Bush.

Commission to Assess United States National Security Space Management and Organization

PO BOX 33633
WASHINGTON DC 20033-0633

Hon. Donald H. Rumsfeld *
Chairman

Hon. Duane P. Andrews	Gen. Charles A. Horner, USAF (Ret.)
Mr. Robert V. Davis	ADM David E. Jeremiah, USN (Ret.)
Gen. Howell M. Estes, III, USAF (Ret.)	Gen. Thomas S. Moorman, Jr., USAF (Ret.)
Gen. Ronald R. Fogleman, USAF (Ret.)	Mr. Douglas H. Necessary
LTG Jay M. Garner, USA (Ret.)	GEN Glenn K. Otis, USA (Ret.)
Hon. William R. Graham	Sen. Malcolm Wallop (ret.)

January 11, 2001

The Honorable Tom Daschle
Majority Leader
United States Senate
Washington, DC 20515

Dear Senator Daschle:

In accordance with section 1623 of the National Defense Authorization Act for Fiscal Year 2000 (P.L. 106-65), we hereby submit the report of the Commission to Assess United States National Security Space Management and Organization. The Commission's report is unanimous. It has been an honor to serve.

Respectfully submitted,

Duane P. Andrews

Robert V. Davis

Howell M. Estes, III

Ronald R. Fogleman

Jay M. Garner

William R. Graham

Charles A. Horner

David E. Jeremiah

Thomas S. Moorman, Jr.

Douglas H. Necessary

Glenn K. Otis

Malcolm Wallop

---

* The Honorable Donald H. Rumsfeld served as a member and chairman of the Commission from its inception until December 28, 2000, when he was nominated for the position of Secretary of Defense by President-elect George W. Bush.

Commission to Assess United States National Security Space Management and Organization

PO BOX 33633
WASHINGTON DC 20033-0633

Hon. Donald H. Rumsfeld *
Chairman

Hon. Duane P. Andrews
Mr. Robert V. Davis
Gen. Howell M. Estes, III, USAF (Ret.)
Gen. Ronald R. Fogleman, USAF (Ret.)
LTG Jay M. Garner, USA (Ret.)
Hon. William R. Graham

Gen. Charles A. Horner, USAF (Ret.)
ADM David E. Jeremiah, USN (Ret.)
Gen. Thomas S. Moorman, Jr., USAF (Ret.)
Mr. Douglas H. Necessary
GEN Glenn K. Otis, USA (Ret.)
Sen. Malcolm Wallop (ret.)

January 11, 2001

The Honorable Trent Lott
Minority Leader
United States Senate
Washington, DC 20515

Dear Senator Lott:

In accordance with section 1623 of the National Defense Authorization Act for Fiscal Year 2000 (P.L. 106-65), we hereby submit the report of the Commission to Assess United States National Security Space Management and Organization. The Commission's report is unanimous. It has been an honor to serve.

Respectfully submitted,

Duane P. Andrews   Robert V. Davis   Howell M. Estes, III

Ronald R. Fogleman   Jay M. Garner   William R. Graham

Charles A. Horner   David E. Jeremiah   Thomas S. Moorman, Jr.

Douglas H. Necessary   Glenn K. Otis   Malcolm Wallop

---

* The Honorable Donald H. Rumsfeld served as a member and chairman of the Commission from its inception until December 28, 2000, when he was nominated for the position of Secretary of Defense by President-elect George W. Bush.

Commission to Assess United States National Security Space Management and Organization

PO BOX 33633
WASHINGTON DC 20033-0633

Hon. Donald H. Rumsfeld *
Chairman

Hon. Duane P. Andrews	Gen. Charles A. Horner, USAF (Ret.)
Mr. Robert V. Davis	ADM David E. Jeremiah, USN (Ret.)
Gen. Howell M. Estes, III, USAF (Ret.)	Gen. Thomas S. Moorman, Jr., USAF (Ret.)
Gen. Ronald R. Fogleman, USAF (Ret.)	Mr. Douglas H. Necessary
LTG Jay M. Garner, USA (Ret.)	GEN Glenn K. Otis, USA (Ret.)
Hon. William R. Graham	Sen. Malcolm Wallop (ret.)

January 11, 2001

The Honorable William S. Cohen
Secretary of Defense
1000 Defense Pentagon
Washington, DC 20301-1000

Dear Mr. Secretary:

In accordance with section 1623 of the National Defense Authorization Act for Fiscal Year 2000 (P.L. 106-65), we hereby submit the report of the Commission to Assess United States National Security Space Management and Organization. The Commission's report is unanimous. It has been an honor to serve.

Respectfully submitted,

Duane P. Andrews   Robert V. Davis   Howell M. Estes, III

Ronald R. Fogleman   Jay M. Garner   William R. Graham

Charles A. Horner   David E. Jeremiah   Thomas S. Moorman, Jr.

Douglas H. Necessary   Glenn K. Otis   Malcolm Wallop

---

* The Honorable Donald H. Rumsfeld served as a member and chairman of the Commission from its inception until December 28, 2000, when he was nominated for the position of Secretary of Defense by President-elect George W. Bush.

Members of the Commission to Assess United States National Security Space Management and Organization

were appointed
by the

Chairman of the Committee on Armed Services of the
United States House of Representatives

Chairman of the Committee on Armed Services of the
United States Senate

Ranking Minority Members of the
Committee on Armed Services of the United States House of Representatives
and the Committee on Armed Services of the United States Senate

Secretary of Defense, in consultation with the
Director of Central Intelligence

The Honorable Duane P. Andrews
Mr. Robert V. Davis
General Howell M. Estes, III, USAF (Ret.)
General Ronald R. Fogleman, USAF (Ret.)
Lieutenant General Jay M. Garner, U.S. Army (Ret.)
The Honorable William R. Graham
General Charles A. Horner, USAF (Ret.)
Admiral David E. Jeremiah, USN (Ret.)
General Thomas S. Moorman, Jr., USAF (Ret.)
Mr. Douglas H. Necessary
General Glenn K. Otis, U.S. Army (Ret.)
The Honorable Donald H. Rumsfeld*
Senator Malcolm Wallop (ret.)

---

* The Honorable Donald H. Rumsfeld served as a member and chairman of the Commission from its inception until December 28, 2000, when he was nominated for the position of Secretary of Defense by President-elect George W. Bush.

Table of Contents

Executive Summary vii

I. **The Commission's Charter** 1
    A. Statutory Charter of the Commission 1
    B. Scope of the Commission's Assessment 2
    C. Organization of the Report 6

II. **Space: Today and the Future** 9
    A. A New Era of Space 9
        1. The Role for Space 10
        2. Toward the Future 17
    B. Vulnerabilities and Threats 17
        1. Assessing the Threat Environment 18
        2. Existing and Emerging Threats 19
        3. Reducing Vulnerability 22

III. **U.S. Objectives for Space** 27
    A. Transform U.S. Military Capabilities 28
        1. Deterrence and Defense Policy for Space 28
        2. Assured Access to Space and On-Orbit Operations 29
        3. Space Situational Awareness 31
        4. Earth Surveillance From Space 31
        5. Global Command, Control and Communications in Space 32
        6. Defense in Space 32
        7. Homeland Defense 32
        8. Power Projection In, From and Through Space 33

- B. Strengthen Intelligence Capabilities 33
  1. Tasks of the Intelligence Community 33
  2. Revolutionary Collection Methods 34
  3. Leveraging Commercial Products 35
- C. Shape the International Legal and
  Regulatory Environment 36
  1. Impact on the Military Use of Space 36
  2. Satellite Regulation 38
- D. Advance U.S. Technological Leadership 39
  1. Investment in Research and Development 40
  2. Government/Industry Relationships 40
  3. New Approaches to Space 41
- E. Create and Sustain a Cadre of Space Professionals 42
  1. Developing a Military Space Culture 42
  2. Professional Military Education 46
  3. Science and Engineering Workforce 47

IV. **Organizations that Affect National Security Space** 49
- A. Executive Office of the President 49
- B. Department of Defense 50
  1. Secretary of Defense 50
  2. Office of the Secretary of Defense 51
  3. Military Commanders in Chief (CINCs) 54
  4. Commander in Chief of U.S. Space Command and North American Aerospace Defense Command and Commander, Air Force Space Command 54
  5. Military Services 55
  6. National Reconnaissance Office 59
- C. Intelligence Community 60
- D. Congress 61

V.	**Management of National Security Space Activities** 63	
	A. Interagency Coordination 63	
	1. Current Interagency Process 63	
	2. Pending Agenda 63	
	B. SecDef/DCI Relationship 64	
	C. Acquiring and Operating Space Systems 65	
	1. Budgeting 66	
	2. Satellite Acquistion 66	
	3. Satellite Operations 67	
	4. Integrated Acquisition and Operations 68	
	D. Pursuing "Leap Ahead" Technologies 68	
	1. Managing Science and Technology Programs 69	
	2. Space Technology Goals 70	
	E. Leveraging the Commercial and Civil Sectors 71	
	1. Launch Facilities 73	
	2. Export Control Policy 73	
	3. Satellite Services 74	
	4. Multinational Space Alliances 75	
	F. Budgeting for Space 75	
	1. Major Force Program 76	
	2. Space Appropriation 76	
	G. Exercises, Experiments and Wargames 77	
	1. Exercises 77	
	2. Experiments 77	
	3. Wargames 78	
	4. Models and Simulation 78	

VI.	Organizing and Managing for the Future	79
	A. Criteria	79
	B. Assessment of Congressionally Directed Approaches	80
	1. A New Military Department for Space	80
	2. Space Corps	81
	3. Assistant Secretary of Defense for Space	81
	4. Major Force Program	82
	C. Recommendations: A New Approach to Space Organization and Management	82
	1. Presidential Leadership	82
	2. Presidential Space Advisory Group	83
	3. Senior Interagency Group for Space	84
	4. SecDef/DCI Relationship	85
	5. Under Secretary of Defense for Space, Intelligence and Information	85
	6. Commander in Chief of U.S. Space Command and NORAD and Commander, Air Force Space Command	87
	7. Military Services	89
	8. Aligning Air Force and NRO Space Programs	90
	9. Innovative Research and Development	95
	10. Budgeting for Space	96
	11. Congress	98
VII.	Conclusions of the Commission	99
VIII.	Attachments	
	A. Résumés of Commission Members	A-1
	B. Résumés of Core Staff of the Commission	B-1
	C. Commission Meetings	C-1
	D. Acknowledgements	D-1
	E. Glossary for Organization Charts	E-1

Executive Summary

A. Conclusions of the Commission

The Commission was directed to assess the organization and management of space activities in support of U.S. national security. Members of the Commission were appointed by the chairmen and ranking minority members of the House and Senate Armed Services Committees and by the Secretary of Defense in consultation with the Director of Central Intelligence.

The Commission unanimously concluded that the security and well being of the United States, its allies and friends depend on the nation's ability to operate in space.

Therefore, it is in the U.S. national interest to:

- Promote the peaceful use of space.

- Use the nation's potential in space to support its domestic, economic, diplomatic and national security objectives.

- Develop and deploy the means to deter and defend against hostile acts directed at U.S. space assets and against the uses of space hostile to U.S. interests.

The pursuit of U.S. national interests in space requires leadership by the President and senior officials. The Commission recommends an early review and, as appropriate, revision of the national space policy. The policy should provide direction and guidance for the departments and agencies of the U.S. Government to:

- Employ space systems to help speed the transformation of the U.S. military into a modern force able to deter and defend against evolving threats directed at the U.S. homeland, its forward deployed forces, allies and interests abroad and in space.

- Develop revolutionary methods of collecting intelligence from space to provide the President the information necessary for him to direct the nation's affairs, manage crises and resolve conflicts in a complex and changing international environment.

Executive Summary

- Shape the domestic and international legal and regulatory environment for space in ways that ensure U.S. national security interests and enhance the competitiveness of the commercial sector and the effectiveness of the civil space sector.

- Promote government and commercial investment in leading edge technologies to assure that the U.S. has the means to master operations in space and compete in international markets.

- Create and sustain within the government a trained cadre of military and civilian space professionals.

The U.S. Government is increasingly dependent on the commercial space sector to provide essential services for national security operations. Those services include satellite communications as well as images of the earth useful to government officials, intelligence analysts and military commanders. To assure the United States remains the world's leading space-faring nation, the government has to become a more reliable consumer of U.S. space products and services and should:

- Invest in technologies to permit the U.S. Government to field systems one generation ahead of what is available commercially to meet unique national security requirements.

- Encourage the U.S. commercial space industry to field systems one generation ahead of international competitors.

The relative dependence of the U.S. on space makes its space systems potentially attractive targets. Many foreign nations and non-state entities are pursuing space-related activities. Those hostile to the U.S. possess, or can acquire on the global market, the means to deny, disrupt or destroy U.S. space systems by attacking satellites in space, communications links to and from the ground or ground stations that command the satellites and process their data. Therefore, the U.S. must develop and maintain intelligence collection capabilities and an analysis approach that will enable it to better understand the intentions and motivations as well as the capabilities of potentially hostile states and entities.

An attack on elements of U.S. space systems during a crisis or conflict should not be considered an improbable act. If the U.S. is to avoid a "Space Pearl Harbor" it needs to take seriously the possibility of an attack on U.S.

space systems. The nation's leaders must assure that the vulnerability of the United States is reduced and that the consequences of a surprise attack on U.S. space assets are limited in their effects.

The Commission has unanimously concluded that organizational and management changes are needed for the following reasons.

> **First, the present extent of U.S. dependence on space, the rapid pace at which this dependence is increasing and the vulnerabilities it creates, all demand that U.S. national security space interests be recognized as a top national security priority. The only way they will receive this priority is through specific guidance and direction from the very highest government levels. Only the President has the authority, first, to set forth the national space policy, and then to provide the guidance and direction to senior officials, that together are needed to ensure that the United States remains the world's leading space-faring nation. Only Presidential leadership can ensure the cooperation needed from all space sectors—commercial, civil, defense and intelligence.**
>
> **Second, the U.S. Government—in particular, the Department of Defense and the Intelligence Community—is not yet arranged or focused to meet the national security space needs of the 21st century. Our growing dependence on space, our vulnerabilities in space and the burgeoning opportunities from space are simply not reflected in the present institutional arrangements. After examining a variety of organizational approaches, the Commission concluded that a number of disparate space activities should promptly be merged, chains of command adjusted, lines of communication opened and policies modified to achieve greater responsibility and accountability. Only then can the necessary trade-offs be made, the appropriate priorities be established and the opportunities for improving U.S. military and intelligence capabilities be realized. Only with senior-level leadership, when properly managed and with the right priorities will U.S. space programs both deserve and attract the funding that is required.**

Third, U.S. national security space programs are vital to peace and stability, and the two officials primarily responsible and accountable for those programs are the Secretary of Defense and the Director of Central Intelligence. Their relationship is critical to the development and deployment of the space capabilities needed to support the President in war, in crisis and also in peace. They must work closely and effectively together, in partnership, both to set and maintain the course for national security space programs and to resolve the differences that arise between their respective bureaucracies. Only if they do so will the armed forces, the Intelligence Community and the National Command Authorities have the information they need to pursue our deterrence and defense objectives successfully in this complex, changing and still dangerous world.

Fourth, we know from history that every medium—air, land and sea—has seen conflict. Reality indicates that space will be no different. Given this virtual certainty, the U.S. must develop the means both to deter and to defend against hostile acts in and from space. This will require superior space capabilities. Thus far, the broad outline of U.S. national space policy is sound, but the U.S. has not yet taken the steps necessary to develop the needed capabilities and to maintain and ensure continuing superiority.

Finally, investment in science and technology resources—not just facilities, but people—is essential if the U.S. is to remain the world's leading space-faring nation. The U.S. Government needs to play an active, deliberate role in expanding and deepening the pool of military and civilian talent in science, engineering and systems operations that the nation will need. The government also needs to sustain its investment in enabling and breakthrough technologies in order to maintain its leadership in space.

B. Space: Today and the Future

With the dramatic and still accelerating advances in science and technology, the use of space is increasing rapidly. Yet, the uses and benefits of space often go unrecognized. We live in an information age, driven by needs for precision, accuracy and timeliness in all of our endeavors—personal, business and governmental. As society becomes increasingly mobile and global, reliance on the worldwide availability of information will increase. Space-based systems, transmitting data, voice and video, will continue to play a critical part in collecting and distributing information. Space is also a medium in which highly valuable applications are being developed and around which highly lucrative economic endeavors are being built.

1. A New Era of Space

The first era of the space age was one of experimentation and discovery. Telstar, Mercury and Apollo, Voyager and Hubble, and the Space Shuttle taught Americans how to journey into space and allowed them to take the first tentative steps toward operating in space while enlarging their knowledge of the universe. We are now on the threshold of a new era of the space age, devoted to mastering operations in space.

The Role for Space
Space-based technology is revolutionizing major aspects of commercial and social activity and will continue to do so as the capacity and capabilities of satellites increase through emerging technologies. Space enters homes, businesses, schools, hospitals and government offices through its applications for transportation, health, the environment, telecommunications, education, commerce, agriculture and energy. Much like highways and airways, water lines and electric grids, services supplied from space are already an important part of the U.S. and global infrastructures.

Space-related capabilities help national leaders to implement American foreign policy and, when necessary, to use military power in ways never before possible. Because of space capabilities, the U.S. is better able to sustain and extend deterrence to its allies and friends in our highly complex international environment.

In the coming period, the U.S. will conduct operations to, from, in and through space in support of its national interests both on the earth and in space. As with national capabilities in the air, on land and at sea, the U.S. must have the capabilities to defend its space assets against hostile acts and to negate the hostile use of space against U.S. interests.

Intelligence collected from space remains essential to U.S. national security. It is essential to the formulation of foreign and defense policies, the capacity of the President to manage crises and conflicts, the conduct of

Executive Summary

military operations and the development of military capabilities to assure the attainment of U.S. objectives. The Department of Defense and the Intelligence Community are undertaking substantial and expensive programs to replace virtually their entire inventory of satellites over the next decade or so. These programs are estimated to cost more than $60 billion during this period.

Opportunities in space are not limited to the United States. Many countries either conduct or participate in space programs dedicated to a variety of tasks, including communications and remote sensing. The U.S. will be tested over time by competing programs or attempts to restrict U.S. space activities through international regulations.

> *The Department of Defense and the Intelligence Community are undertaking...expensive programs to replace virtually their entire inventory of satellites...*

Toward the Future

Mastering near-earth space operations is still in its early stages. As mastery over operating in space is achieved, the value of activity in space will grow. Commercial space activity will become increasingly important to the global economy. Civil activity will involve more nations, international consortia and non-state actors. U.S. defense and intelligence activities in space will become increasingly important to the pursuit of U.S. national security interests.

The Commissioners appreciate the sensitivity that surrounds the notion of weapons in space for offensive or defensive purposes. They also believe, however, that to ignore the issue would be a disservice to the nation. The Commissioners believe the U.S. Government should vigorously pursue the capabilities called for in the National Space Policy to ensure that the President will have the option to deploy weapons in space to deter threats to and, if necessary, defend against attacks on U.S. interests.

2. Vulnerabilities and Threats

Space systems are vulnerable to a range of attacks that could disrupt or destroy the ground stations, launch systems or satellites on orbit. The political, economic and military value of space systems makes them attractive targets for state and non-state actors hostile to the United States and its interests. In order to extend its deterrence concepts and defense capabilities to space, the U.S. will require development of new military capabilities for operation to, from, in and through space. It will require, as well, engaging U.S. allies and friends, and the international community, in a sustained effort to fashion appropriate "rules of the road" for space.

Assessing the Threat Environment

The U.S. is more dependent on space than any other nation. Yet, the threat to the U.S. and its allies in and from space does not command the attention it merits from the departments and agencies of the U.S. Government charged with national security responsibilities. Consequently, evaluation of the threat to U.S. space capabilities currently lacks priority in the competition for collection and analytic resources. Failure to develop credible threat analyses could have serious consequences for the United States. It could leave the U.S. vulnerable to surprises in space and could result in deferred decisions on developing space-based capabilities due to the lack of a validated, well-understood threat.

The ability to restrict or deny freedom of access to and operations in space is no longer limited to global military powers. Knowledge of space systems and the means to counter them is increasingly available on the international market. The reality is that there are many extant capabilities to deny, disrupt or physically destroy space systems and the ground facilities that use and control them. Examples include denial and deception, interference with satellite systems, jamming satellites on orbit, use of microsatellites for hostile action and detonation of a nuclear weapon in space.

> *The U.S. is more dependent on space than any other nation.*

Reducing Vulnerability

As harmful as the loss of commercial satellites or damage to civil assets would be, an attack on intelligence and military satellites would be even more serious for the nation in time of crisis or conflict. As history has shown—whether at Pearl Harbor, the killing of 241 U.S. Marines in their barracks in Lebanon or the attack on the USS Cole in Yemen—if the U.S. offers an inviting target, it may well pay the price of attack. With the growing commercial and national security use of space, U.S. assets in space and on the ground offer just such targets. The U.S. is an attractive candidate for a "Space Pearl Harbor." The warning signs of U.S. vulnerability include:

Executive Summary

- In 1998, the Galaxy IV satellite malfunctioned, shutting down 80 percent of U.S. pagers, as well as video feeds for cable and broadcast transmissions. It took weeks in some cases to fully restore satellite service.

- In early 2000, the U.S. lost all information from a number of its satellites for three hours when computers in ground stations malfunctioned.

- In July 2000, the Xinhua news agency reported that China's military is developing methods and strategies for defeating the U.S. military in a high-tech and space-based future war.

The signs of vulnerability are not always so clear as those described above and therefore are not always recognized. Hostile actions against space systems can reasonably be confused with natural phenomena. Space debris or solar activity can "explain" the loss of a space system and mask unfriendly actions or the potential thereof. Such ambiguity and uncertainty could be fatal to the successful management of a crisis or resolution of a conflict. They could lead to forbearance when action is needed or to hasty action when more or better information would have given rise to a broader and more effective set of response options.

> *The U.S. is an attractive candidate for a "Space Pearl Harbor."*

There are a number of possible crises or conflicts in which the potential vulnerability of national security space systems would be worrisome. For example:

- Efforts to identify and strike terrorist strongholds and facilities in advance of or in retaliation for terrorist attacks on U.S. forces or citizens abroad, or on the U.S. homeland or that of its allies.

- Conflict in the Taiwan Straits, in which the U.S. attempts to deter escalation through the conduct of military operations while seeking to bring it to a favorable end through diplomatic measures.

- War in the Middle East, posing a threat to U.S. friends and allies in the region and calling for a rapid political and military response to threats by an aggressor to launch ballistic missiles armed with weapons of mass destruction.

Executive Summary

That U.S. space systems might be threatened or attacked in such contingencies may seem improbable, even reckless. However, as political economist Thomas Schelling has pointed out, "There is a tendency in our planning to confuse the unfamiliar with the improbable. The contingency we have not considered looks strange; what looks strange is thought improbable; what is improbable need not be considered seriously." Surprise is most often not a lack of warning, but the result of a tendency to dismiss as reckless what we consider improbable.

> *We are on notice, but we have not noticed.*

History is replete with instances in which warning signs were ignored and change resisted until an external, "improbable" event forced resistant bureaucracies to take action. The question is whether the U.S. will be wise enough to act responsibly and soon enough to reduce U.S. space vulnerability. Or whether, as in the past, a disabling attack against the country and its people—a "Space Pearl Harbor"—will be the only event able to galvanize the nation and cause the U.S. Government to act.

We are on notice, but we have not noticed.

C. U.S. Objectives for Space

How the U.S. develops the potential of space for civil, commercial, defense and intelligence purposes will affect the nation's security for decades to come.

> *How the U.S. develops the potential of space for civil, commercial, defense and intelligence purposes will affect the nation's security for decades to come.*

America's interests in space are to:

- Promote the peaceful use of space.

- Use the nation's potential in space to support U.S. domestic, economic, diplomatic and national security objectives.

- Develop and deploy the means to deter and defend against hostile acts directed at U.S. space assets and against the uses of space hostile to U.S. interests.

Executive Summary

The U.S. Government must work actively to make sure that the nation has the means necessary to advance its interests in space. This requires action in the following areas.

1. Transform U.S. Military Capabilities

> *A deterrence strategy for space…must be supported by a greater range of space capabilities.*

The United States must develop, deploy and maintain the means to deter attack on and to defend vulnerable space capabilities. Explicit national security guidance and defense policy is needed to direct development of doctrine, concepts of operations and capabilities for space, including weapons systems that operate in space and that can defend assets in orbit and augment air, land and sea forces. This requires a deterrence strategy for space, which in turn must be supported by a broader range of space capabilities. Improvements are needed in the areas of:

- Assured access to space and on-orbit operations.
- Space situational awareness.
- Earth surveillance from space.
- Global command, control and communications in space.
- Defense in space.
- Homeland defense.
- Power projection in, from and through space.

The senior political and military leadership needs to test these capabilities in exercises on a regular basis. Exercises, including "live fire" events, are needed both to keep the armed forces proficient in the use of these capabilities and to bolster their deterrent effect on potential adversaries. While exercises may give adversaries information they can use to challenge American space capabilities, that risk must be balanced against the fact that capabilities that are untested, unknown or unproven cannot be expected to deter.

2. Strengthen Intelligence Capabilities

The U.S. needs to strengthen its ability to collect information about the activities, capabilities and intentions of potential adversaries and to overcome their efforts to deny the U.S. this information. Since the end of the Cold War, the number, complexity and scope of high-priority tasks assigned to the Intelligence Community have increased even as its human resources and technical advantage have eroded. This has reduced the Intelligence Community's ability to provide timely and accurate estimates of threats and has correspondingly increased the possibility of surprise.

To meet the challenges posed to space-based intelligence collection, the U.S. needs to review its approach to intelligence collection from space. Planned and programmed collection platforms may not be adaptable enough to meet the many and varied tasks assigned. To the extent that commercial products, particularly imagery from U.S. commercial remote sensing companies, can meet intelligence collection needs, these should be incorporated into an overall collection architecture. The U.S. must also invest in space-based collection technologies that will provide revolutionary methods for collecting intelligence.

3. Shape the International Legal and Regulatory Environment

U.S. activity in space, both governmental and commercial, is governed by treaties and by international and domestic law and regulations, which have contributed to the orderly use of space by all nations. As interest in and use of space increases, both within the United States and around the world, the U.S. must participate actively in shaping the space legal and regulatory environment. To protect the country's interests, the U.S. must promote the peaceful use of space, monitor activities of regulatory bodies, and protect the rights of nations to defend their interests in and from space. The U.S. and most other nations interpret "peaceful" to mean "non-aggressive"; this comports with customary international law allowing for routine military activities in outer space, as it does on the high seas and in international airspace. There is no blanket prohibition in international law on placing or using weapons in space, applying force from space to earth or conducting military operations in and through space. The U.S. must be cautious of agreements intended

The U.S. must participate actively in shaping the space legal and regulatory environment.

Executive Summary

for one purpose that, when added to a larger web of treaties or regulations, may have the unintended consequences of restricting future activities in space.

4. Advance U.S. Technological Leadership

To achieve national security objectives and compete successfully internationally, the U.S. must maintain technological leadership in space. This requires a healthy industrial base, improved science and technology resources, an attitude of risk-taking and innovation, and government policies that support international competitiveness. In particular, the government needs to significantly increase its investment in breakthrough technologies to fuel innovative, revolutionary capabilities. Mastery of space also requires new approaches that reduce significantly the cost of building and launching space systems. The U.S. will not remain the world's leading space-faring nation by relying on yesterday's technology to meet today's requirements at tomorrow's prices.

> *The U.S. will not remain the world's leading space-faring nation by relying on yesterday's technology to meet today's requirements at tomorrow's prices.*

5. Create and Sustain a Cadre of Space Professionals

Since its inception, a hallmark of the U.S. space program has been world-class scientists, engineers and operators from academic institutions, industry, government agencies and the military Services. Sustained excellence in the scientific and engineering disciplines is essential to the future of the nation's national security space program. It cannot be taken for granted.

Military space professionals will have to master highly complex technology; develop new doctrine and concepts of operations for space launch, offensive and defensive space operations, power projection in, from and through space and other military uses of space; and operate some of the most complex systems ever built and deployed. To ensure the needed talent and experience, the Department of Defense, the Intelligence Community and the nation as a whole must place a high priority on intensifying investments in career development, education and training to develop and sustain a cadre of highly competent and motivated military and civilian space professionals.

Executive Summary

D. Organizations that Affect National Security Space

The principal organizations involved in national security space include the Executive Office of the President, the Department of Defense, the Intelligence Community and the Congress (Figure 1).

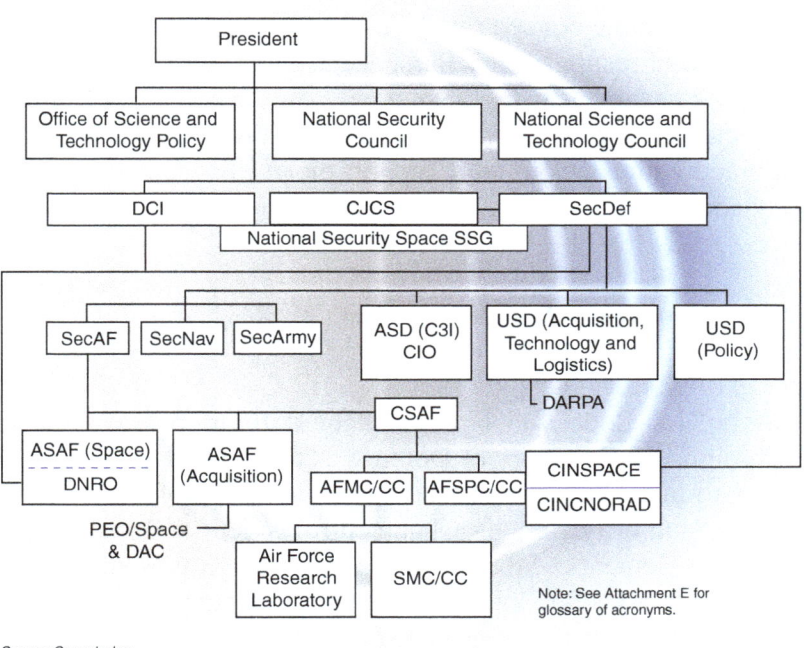

Source: Commission

Figure 1: Current Organization for Managing US National Security Space Activity

1. Executive Office of the President

There is no single individual other than the President who can provide the sustained and deliberate leadership, direction and oversight of national security space policy that is needed. Currently, responsibility and accountability for space are broadly diffused throughout the government.

Executive Summary

The 1996 National Space Policy designates the National Science and Technology Council (NSTC), a Cabinet-level organization chaired by the President, as "the principal forum for resolving issues related to national space policy." The policy directs that, "as appropriate, the NSTC and NSC [National Security Council] will co-chair policy processes." In the National Security Council, national security space issues are currently assigned to the Senior Director for Defense Policy and Arms Control.

This arrangement has not, does not and cannot provide the focused attention to space matters that is needed. The interdependence of the space sectors requires a more concentrated focus on space at the Cabinet level. The distribution of responsibility for space activity among many departments and agencies is less than ideal. Moreover, the portfolio of the Senior Director with responsibility for space affairs on the NSC is broad. That combined with a lack of staff support means that space issues are selectively addressed, most frequently only when they have become crises.

2. Department of Defense

Secretary of Defense

Title 10 of the U.S. Code, which provides the statutory basis for the Armed Services, assigns the Secretary of Defense as the principal assistant to the President in all matters relating to the Department of Defense. The Secretary has "authority, direction, and control" over the Department. With respect to those elements of the Intelligence Community within the Department, Title 50 U.S.C. provides the statutory basis for the Intelligence Community and directs that the Secretary, in consultation with the Director of Central Intelligence (DCI), "shall...ensure that [their] budgets are adequate...[and] ensure appropriate implementation of the policies and resource decisions of the Director of Central Intelligence by [those] elements..." This dual tasking establishes the obligation for the Secretary of Defense to ensure that the missions of the Department of Defense and of the Intelligence Community are successfully completed.

The relationship between the Secretary of Defense and the Director of Central Intelligence has evolved over time in such a manner that national security space issues do not receive the sustained focus appropriate to their importance to national security.

Executive Summary

Office of the Secretary of Defense

Except for responding to urgent programmatic decisions, defense secretaries have generally delegated management of national security space activities. Today, this responsibility is delegated to the Assistant Secretary of Defense for Command, Control, Communications, and Intelligence (ASD (C3I)), who serves as the "principal staff assistant and advisor to the Secretary and Deputy Secretary of Defense and the focal point within the Department for space and space-related activities." The ASD (C3I) in turn relies on deputy assistant secretaries to guide policy and acquisition and provide oversight of the Department's intelligence, surveillance, reconnaissance, information, command, control, communications and space programs.

The current ASD (C3I) organization suffers from three difficulties:

- The span of control is so broad that only the most pressing issues are attended to and space matters are left, on a day-to-day basis, in the hands of middle-level officials without sufficient influence within the Department and the interagency arena.

- Its influence on the planning, programming and budgeting process for space is too far removed or too late to have substantial effect on either the Services' or the Intelligence Community's processes.

- Within this structure it is not possible for senior officials outside DoD to identify a single, high-level individual who has the authority to represent the Department on space-related matters.

Commander in Chief of U.S. Space Command and North American Aerospace Defense Command and Commander, Air Force Space Command

The Commander in Chief, U.S. Space Command (CINCSPACE) serves as the Commander in Chief, North American Aerospace Defense Command (CINCNORAD) and as the Commander, Air Force Space Command. As CINCSPACE, he serves as the advocate for the space requirements for all the CINCs and, on an annual basis, submits to the Chairman of the Joint Chiefs of Staff an Integrated Priority List that reflects these requirements. CINCSPACE has a broad set of responsibilities that are quite different in character. He is responsible for protecting and defending the space environment. His responsibilities also include support of strategic ballistic missile defense and the Department's computer network attack and computer network defense missions.

Executive Summary

With the growing dependence on space and the vulnerability of space-related assets, more attention needs to be given to deploying and employing space-based capabilities for deterrence and defense. As space missions continue to expand, space will continue to mature as an "area of responsibility." All of this will require CINCSPACE to pay more attention to the space tasks assigned by the National Command Authorities, leaving less time for other assigned duties as CINCNORAD and Commander, Air Force Space Command.

Military Services

Each military Service is directed by the Secretary of Defense to execute specific space programs, comply with DoD space policy and integrate space capabilities into its strategy, doctrine, education, training, exercises and operations. Each Service is free to develop those space capabilities needed to perform its mission. However, no single service has been assigned statutory responsibility to "organize, train and equip" for space operations. Eighty-five percent of space-related budget activity within the Department of Defense, approximately $7 billion per year, resides in the Air Force.

Within the Air Force, space-related activity is centered primarily in four elements. Space systems operations and requirements are organized under Air Force Space Command (AFSPC). Design, development and acquisition of space launch, command and control, and satellite systems are conducted by personnel assigned to the Space and Missile Systems Center (SMC) under the Air Force Materiel Command. The Program Executive Officer (PEO) and the SMC Commander, who also serves as the Designated Acquisition Commander (DAC), report to the Assistant Secretary of the Air Force for Acquisition on the cost, schedule and performance for the programs in their portfolios. The Air Force Research Laboratory, also part of Air Force Materiel Command, conducts advanced technology research.

> *As with air operations, the Air Force must take steps to create a culture within the Service dedicated to developing new space system concepts, doctrine and operational capabilities.*

The Commission heard testimony that there is a lack of confidence that the Air Force will fully address the requirement to provide space capabilities for the other Services. Many believe the Air Force treats space solely as a supporting capability that enhances the primary mission of the Air Force to conduct offensive and defensive air operations. Despite official doctrine that calls for the integration of space and air capabilities, the Air Force does not treat the two equally. As with air operations, the Air Force must take steps to create a culture within the Service dedicated to developing new space system concepts, doctrine and operational capabilities.

National Reconnaissance Office

The National Reconnaissance Office (NRO) is the single national organization tasked to meet the U.S. Government's intelligence needs for space-borne reconnaissance. The NRO is responsible for unique and innovative technology; large-scale systems engineering; development, acquisition and operation of space reconnaissance systems; and related intelligence activities needed to support national security missions. While the NRO is an agency of the Department of Defense, its budget, the National Reconnaissance Program (NRP), is one part of the National Foreign Intelligence Program (NFIP). The Director of Central Intelligence provides guidance for and approves the NRP and all other elements of the NFIP. The Secretary of Defense ensures implementation of the DCI's resource decisions by DoD elements within the NFIP. As a result, the NRO is a joint venture between these organizations.

> *The NRO today is a different organization, simultaneously struggling to manage a large number of legacy programs while working to renew a focus on leading edge research.*

The NRO had a reputation as one of the U.S. Government's best system acquisition agencies and worked to maintain exceptional systems engineering capabilities. In its early years, the NRO was a small, agile organization, a leader in developing advanced technologies, often first-of-a-kind systems, for solving some of the nation's most difficult intelligence collection challenges. The NRO today is a different organization, simultaneously struggling to manage a large number of legacy programs while working to renew a focus on leading edge research. The NRO's capacity to convert leading edge research and technology into innovative operational systems is inhibited by the requirement to maintain its legacy programs.

3. Intelligence Community

The Director of Central Intelligence is the principal advisor to the President for intelligence matters related to national security and serves as the head of the Intelligence Community. The DCI is responsible for providing national intelligence to the President, to the heads of departments and

Executive Summary

agencies of the executive branch, to the Chairman of the Joint Chiefs of Staff and senior military commanders and, when appropriate, to the Congress. "National intelligence" refers to "intelligence which pertains to the interests of more than one department or agency of the government."

The DCI develops and presents to the President an annual budget for the National Foreign Intelligence Program, which is distributed throughout the budgets of the various departments and agencies that comprise the Intelligence Community.

The Community Management Staff, managed by the Deputy Director of Central Intelligence for Community Management, assists the DCI in coordinating and managing the Intelligence Community, including responsibility for managing resources and collection requirements and assessing space programs and policies. It is also responsible for coordinating policy and budgets with the Office of the Secretary of Defense. The Community Management Staff has made substantial progress in coordinating the planning and budgeting of the components of the Intelligence Community. However, it does not have authority to reprogram in-year money within components, an authority that would enhance its direction of Intelligence Community affairs. Nor is it well structured to coordinate with OSD on broad intelligence policy, long-term space strategy and other issues requiring intelligence support.

4. Congress

Congressional oversight of the authorization and appropriation of national security space funding routinely involves no fewer than six committees. Generally, each committee mirrors the priorities of the executive branch interests it oversees. Executive branch officials must expend considerable time and energy interacting with a large number of committees and subcommittees that, on some matters, have overlapping jurisdiction. To the extent that this process can be streamlined, it would likely benefit the nation, Congress and the executive branch. It would also help if there were an environment in which national security space matters could be addressed as an integrated program—one that includes consideration for commercial and civil capabilities that are often overlooked today.

This report offers suggestions for organizational changes in the executive branch that are intended to bring a more focused, well-directed approach to the conduct of national security space activities, based on a clear national space policy directed by the President. These organizational changes in the executive branch suggest changes in the Congressional committee and subcommittee structure to align the jurisdictions of these committees as much as possible with the executive branch, leading to a more streamlined process. Congress might usefully consider encouraging greater "crossover" membership among all of the space-related committees to increase legislative coordination between defense and intelligence space programs.

E. Management of National Security Space Activities

A number of issues transcend organizational approaches and are important to the ability of the U.S. to achieve its objectives in space. These are issues that the national leadership, the Department of Defense and the Intelligence Community should address in the near term irrespective of particular organizational arrangements that may be pursued.

1. Interagency Coordination

The present interagency process is inadequate for the volume and complexity of today's space issues. For the most part, the existing interagency process addresses space issues on an as needed basis. As issues in the space arena inevitably become more complex, this approach will become increasingly unsatisfactory. What may be needed is a standing interagency group to identify key national security space issues, to guide, as necessary, the revision of existing national space policy and to oversee implementation of that policy throughout the departments and agencies of the U.S. Government. The need for a standing interagency coordination process is made more urgent by the fact that there are a number of pending issues on space affairs in Congress, in domestic regulatory bodies and in international trade and arms control negotiating fora. To avoid unintended and deleterious effects on the space sectors, these issues must be addressed in a comprehensive fashion.

2. SecDef/DCI Relationship

No relationship within the executive branch touching on national security space is as important as the one between the Secretary of Defense and the Director of Central Intelligence. Together, the Secretary and the DCI control national security space capabilities. Neither can accomplish the

Executive Summary

tasks assigned without the support of the other. The Secretary and the DCI have not given the national security space program their sustained, joint attention for nearly a decade. Nor have the urgent issues related to space control, information operations and the assessment of the threats the nation faces from space received the attention they deserve. The Secretary and the DCI need to align their respective staff offices so that coordination on intelligence issues broadly, and space matters specifically, is easier and more direct between the two.

> *No relationship…touching on national security space is as important as the one between the Secretary of Defense and the Director of Central Intelligence.*

3. Acquiring and Operating Space Systems

The Department of Defense and the Intelligence Community acquire and operate most of the satellites used to support defense and intelligence missions. Within DoD, the Air Force is the Service that acquires most of the Department's satellites; the NRO is the acquisition agent for the Intelligence Community's space systems. The acquisition processes used by DoD and the NRO have become similar in recent years. The NRO relies on authorities delegated by both the Secretary of Defense and the Director of the Central Intelligence Agency. By virtue of these authorities, the NRO is able, for some purposes unique to its mission, to award and administer contracts without a number of the encumbrances that affect DoD. Because the use of NRO and Air Force satellites is sufficiently different, the approach to operations in the two organizations is also different in character.

The NRO's approach to acquisition and operations, referred to as "cradle-to-grave," creates a different relationship between the acquirers and operators than that of the Air Force, in which the acquisition and operations elements are in separate commands. With the NRO model, the same individuals are involved in the acquisition and operations processes. Therefore, the experiences and understanding derived from operations can more directly influence satellite design. This is not the case in the Air Force, where the operators have less direct influence. When the operators are on the technical design team, their capacity to resolve on-orbit anomalies is also greater. These differences amount, in essence, to different organizational cultures within NRO and Air Force space activities, an understanding of which is essential to determining whether and how the activities might be integrated over time.

Executive Summary

4. Pursuing "Leap Ahead" Technologies

Technological superiority has aided the U.S. military in maintaining its worldwide commitments even as the size of its force has been reduced. As the spread of high technology weaponry on the world market continues, it will become increasingly difficult to stay ahead, particularly in space-related technologies. The Department of Defense needs to provide both resources and direction to ensure that advances in space technology continue. In addition to establishing possible areas for investment, the Department, in cooperation with the space community, needs to ensure that an environment exists within which experimentation and innovation will flourish. The Department also needs to actively coordinate science and technology investments across the space technology community so as to better integrate and prioritize these efforts, many of which have application across all space sectors. And, finally, it needs to encourage demonstration projects, such as Discoverer II was planned to be, if the U.S. is to develop and deploy effective, affordable systems dedicated to military missions in space.

5. Leveraging the Commercial and Civil Sectors

Despite the importance of the U.S. commercial and civil space sectors to the successful completion of the national security mission, the U.S. Government has no comprehensive approach to incorporating these capabilities and services into its national security space architecture. The U.S. Government, as a consumer, a regulator or an investor, is currently not a good partner to the national security space industry. To ensure support for the commercial and civil sectors, the U.S. Government must:

> *The U.S. Government, as a consumer, a regulator or an investor, is currently not a good partner to the national security space industry.*

- Use more expeditious licensing processes while safeguarding U.S. national security interests.

- Develop a strategy for integrating and funding commercial services to meet, as practical, part of current and future national security space requirements.

Executive Summary

- Develop a strategy for relying more on commercial launch facilities, toward the goal of largely privatizing the national launch infrastructure.

- Foster multinational alliances to help maintain the U.S. position as a leader in the global space market.

6. Budgeting for Space

Currently, there is no DoD appropriation that identifies and aggregates funding for space programs. Space funding is a part of many appropriations spread across the DoD and Intelligence Community budgets. Most of the funding for national security space is in the Air Force and National Reconnaissance Office budgets. The Army and Navy each fund space programs that are primarily in support of Service-unique requirements. In the Navy's case, funding supports satellite communication and satellite surveillance systems.

These multiple appropriations lead to several problems. When satellite programs are funded in one budget and terminals in another, the decentralized arrangement can result in program disconnects and duplication. It can result in lack of synchronization in the acquisition of satellites and their associated terminals. It can also be difficult for user requirements to be incorporated into the satellite system if the organization funding the system does not agree with and support those user requirements. The current methods of budgeting for national security space programs lack the visibility and accountability essential to developing a coherent program.

Looking to the future, the Department of Defense will undertake new responsibilities in space, including deterrence and defense of space-based assets as well as other defense and power projection missions in and from space. These new missions will require development of new systems and capabilities. Space capabilities are not funded at a level commensurate with their relative importance. Nor is there a plan in place to build up to the investments needed to modernize existing systems and procure new capabilities. Appropriate investments in space-based capabilities would enable the Department to pursue:

Executive Summary

- Improved space situational awareness and attack warning capabilities.

- Enhanced protection/defensive measures, prevention and negation systems and rapid long-range power projection capabilities.

- Modernized launch capabilities.

- A more robust science and technology program for developing and deploying space-based radar, space-based laser, hyper-spectral sensors and reusable launch vehicle technology.

Providing the Department of Defense and the Intelligence Community with additional resources to accomplish these new missions should be considered as part of U.S. national space policy.

7. Exercises, Experiments and Wargames

The military uses a variety of tools to simulate warfighting environments in support of exercises, experiments and wargames. However, these tools have not been modernized to take into account the missions and tasks that space systems can perform. As a result, simulation tools cannot be used effectively to understand the utility of space-based capabilities on warfare. Further, the lack of modeling and simulation tools has prevented military commanders from learning how to cope with the loss or temporary interruption of key space capabilities, such as the Global Positioning System (GPS), satellite communications, remote sensing or missile warning information. To support exercises, experiments and wargames, the Department must develop and employ modeling and simulation tools based on measures of merit and effectiveness that will quantify the effects of space-based capabilities.

F. Recommendations: Organizing and Managing for the Future

National security space organization and management today fail to reflect the growing importance of space to U.S. interests. There is a need for greater emphasis on space-related matters, starting at the highest levels of government.

> *National security space organization and management today fail to reflect the growing importance of space to U.S. interests.*

Executive Summary

In light of the vital place space has in the spectrum of national security interests, a successful approach to organization and management for the future must:

- Provide for national-level guidance that establishes space activity as a fundamental national interest of the United States.

- Create a process to ensure that the national-level policy guidance is carried out among and within the relevant agencies and departments.

- Ensure the government's ability to participate effectively in shaping the domestic and international rules and policies that will govern space.

- Create conditions that encourage the Department of Defense to develop and deploy systems in space to deter attack on and, if deterrence should fail, to defend U.S. interests on earth and in space.

- Create conditions that encourage the Intelligence Community to develop revolutionary methods for collecting intelligence from space.

- Provide methods for resolving the inevitable issues between the defense and intelligence sectors on the priority, funding and control of space programs.

- Account for the increasingly important role played by the commercial and civil space sectors in the nation's domestic and global economic and national security affairs.

- Develop a military and civilian cadre of space professionals within DoD, the Intelligence Community and throughout government more generally.

- Provide an organizational and management structure that permits officials to be agile in addressing the opportunities, risks and threats that inevitably will arise.

- Ensure that DoD and the Intelligence Community are full participants in preparing government positions for international negotiations that may affect U.S. space activities.

The Commission believes that a new and more comprehensive approach is needed to further the nation's security interests in space (Figure 2).

Executive Summary

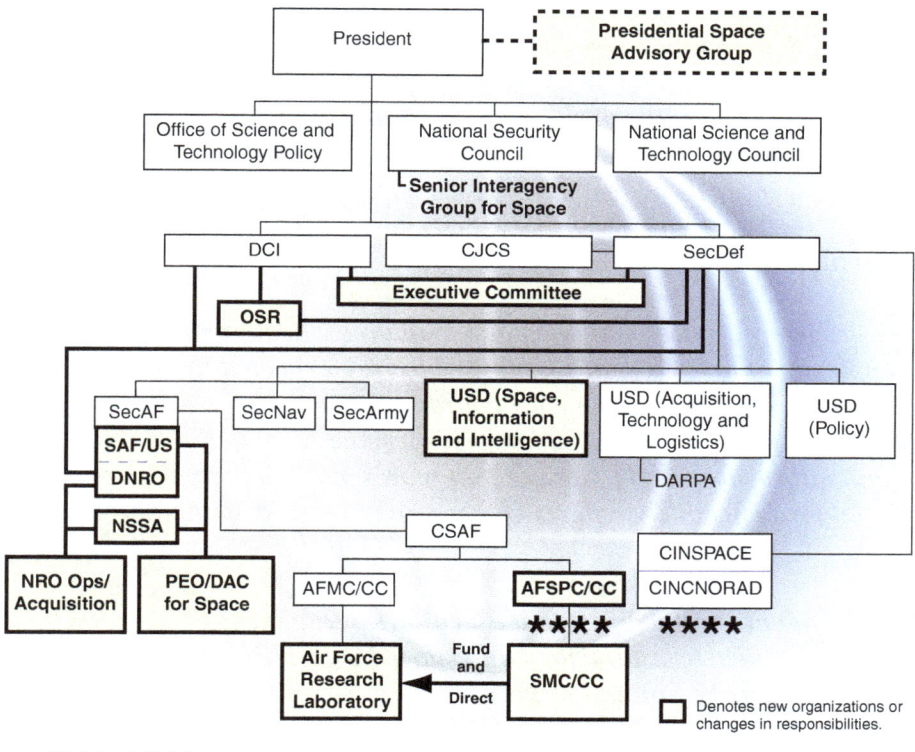

Source: Commission

Figure 2: A New Organizational Approach for Space

Following are the Commission's unanimous recommendations.

1. Presidential Leadership

The United States has a vital national interest in space. National security space should be high among the nation's priorities. It deserves the attention of the national leadership, from the President down.

> **The President should consider establishing space as a national security priority.**

2. Presidential Space Advisory Group

The President might find it useful to have access to high-level advice in developing a long-term strategy for sustaining the nation's role as the leading space-faring nation.

xxxi

Executive Summary

> *The President should consider the appointment of a Presidential Space Advisory Group to provide independent advice on developing and employing new space capabilities.*

3. Senior Interagency Group for Space

The current interagency process is inadequate to address the number, range and complexity of today's space issues, which are expected to increase over time. A standing interagency coordination process is needed to focus on policy formulation and coordination of space activities pertinent to national security and to assure that representation in domestic and international fora effectively reflects U.S. national security and other space interests.

> *The President should direct that a Senior Interagency Group for Space be established and staffed within the National Security Council structure.*

4. SecDef/DCI Relationship

The issues relating to space between the Department of Defense and the Intelligence Community are sufficiently numerous and complex that their successful resolution and implementation require a close, continuing and effective relationship between the Secretary of Defense and the Director of Central Intelligence.

> *The Secretary of Defense and the Director of Central Intelligence should meet regularly to address national security space policy, objectives and issues.*

5. Under Secretary of Defense for Space, Intelligence and Information

Until space organizations have more fully evolved, the Office of the Secretary of Defense would benefit from having a senior-level official with sufficient standing to serve as the advocate for space within the Department. The Secretary of Defense would assign this official responsibility to oversee the Department's research and development, acquisition, launch and operation of its space, intelligence and information assets; coordinate the military intelligence activities within the Department; and work with the Intelligence Community on long-range intelligence requirements for national security.

> **An Under Secretary of Defense for Space, Intelligence and Information should be established.**

6. Commander in Chief of U.S. Space Command and NORAD and Commander, Air Force Space Command

The Commander in Chief, U.S. Space Command should continue to concentrate on space as it relates to warfare in the mediums of air, land and sea, as well as space. His primary role is to conduct space operations and provide space-related services, to include computer network defense/ attack missions in support of the operations of the other CINCs, and national missile defense. This broad and varied set of responsibilities as CINCSPACE will leave less time for his other assigned duties.

> **The Secretary of the Air Force should assign responsibility for the command of Air Force Space Command to a four-star officer other than CINCSPACE/CINCNORAD.**

> **The Secretary of Defense should end the practice of assigning only Air Force flight-rated officers to the position of CINCSPACE and CINCNORAD to ensure that an officer from any Service with an understanding of combat and space could be assigned to this position.**

7. Military Services

The Department of Defense requires space systems that can be employed in independent operations or in support of air, land and sea forces to deter and defend against hostile actions directed at the interests of the United States. In the mid term a Space Corps within the Air Force may be appropriate to meet this requirement; in the longer term it may be met by a military department for space. In the nearer term, a realigned, rechartered Air Force is best suited to organize, train and equip space forces.

Executive Summary

> *The Air Force should realign headquarters and field commands to more effectively organize, train and equip for prompt and sustained space operations. Assign Air Force Space Command (AFSPC) responsibility for providing the resources to execute space research, development, acquisition and operations, under the command of a four-star general. The Army and Navy would still establish requirements and develop and deploy space systems unique to each Service.*

> *Amend Title 10 U.S.C. to assign the Air Force responsibility to organize, train and equip for prompt and sustained offensive and defensive air <u>and</u> space operations. In addition, the Secretary of Defense should designate the Air Force as Executive Agent for Space within the Department of Defense.*

8. Aligning Air Force and NRO Space Programs

The Department of Defense and the Intelligence Community would benefit from the appointment of a single official within the Air Force with authority for the acquisition of space systems for the Air Force and the NRO based on the "best practices" of each organization.

> *Assign the Under Secretary of the Air Force as the Director of the National Reconnaissance Office. Designate the Under Secretary as the Air Force Acquisition Executive for Space.*

9. Innovative Research and Development

The Intelligence Community has a need for revolutionary methods, including but not limited to space systems, for collecting intelligence.

> *The Secretary of Defense and the Director of Central Intelligence should direct the creation of a research, development and demonstration organization to focus on this requirement.*

Competitive centers of innovation that actively pursue space-related research, development and demonstration programs are desirable.

> **The Secretary of Defense should direct the Defense Advanced Research Projects Agency and the Services' laboratories to undertake development and demonstration of innovative space technologies and systems for dedicated military missions.**

10. Budgeting for Space

Better visibility into the level and distribution of fiscal and personnel resources would improve management and oversight of space programs.

> **The Secretary of Defense should establish a Major Force Program for Space.**

The Commission believes that its recommendations, taken as a whole, will enable the U.S. to sustain its position as the world's leading space-faring nation. Presidential leadership and guidance, coupled with a more effective interagency process and especially with improved coordination between the Department of Defense and the Intelligence Community, are essential if the nation is to promote and protect its interests in space.

I. The Commission's Charter

A. Statutory Charter of the Commission

The Commission to Assess United States National Security Space Management and Organization was established pursuant to Public Law 106-65, the National Defense Authorization Act for Fiscal Year 2000, Section 1622.

The mandate is as follows:

"The Commission shall, concerning changes to be implemented over the near-term, medium-term and long-term that would strengthen United States national security, assess the following:

(1) The manner in which military space assets may be exploited to provide support for United States military operations.

(2) The current interagency coordination process regarding the operation of national security space assets, including identification of interoperability and communications issues.

(3) The relationship between the intelligence and nonintelligence aspects of national security space…and the potential costs and benefits of a partial or complete merger of the programs, projects, or activities that are differentiated by those two aspects.

(4) The manner in which military space issues are addressed by professional military education institutions.

(5) The potential costs and benefits of establishing:

   (A) An independent military department and service dedicated to the national security space mission.

   (B) A corps within the Air Force dedicated to the national security space mission.

   (C) A position of Assistant Secretary of Defense for Space within the Office of the Secretary of Defense.

The Commission's Charter

    (D) A new major force program, or other budget mechanism, for managing national security space funding within the Department of Defense.

    (E) Any other change in the existing organizational structure of the Department of Defense for national security space management and organization."

The National Defense Authorization Act for Fiscal Year 2001 amended the Commission mandate, adding the following task:

(6) "The advisability of

    (A) various actions to eliminate the requirement for specified officers in the United States Space Command to be flight rated that results from the dual assignment of such officers to that command and to one or more other commands for which the officers are expressly required to be flight rated;

    (B) the establishment of a requirement that all new general or flag officers of the United States Space Command have experience in space, missile, or information operations that is either acquisition experience or operational experience; and

    (C) rotating the command of the United States Space Command among the Armed Forces."

B. Scope of the Commission's Assessment

> *The U.S. has an urgent interest in promoting and protecting the peaceful use of space...*

The Commission's charter was to assess the organization and management of space activities that support U.S. national security interests. (Figure 3 represents the U.S. Government organizations currently involved in space activities.) The Commission took into account the range of space missions and functions identified in the 1996 National Space Policy, but focused its assessment on national security space activity. As a result, attention was given primarily to the Department of Defense (DoD)

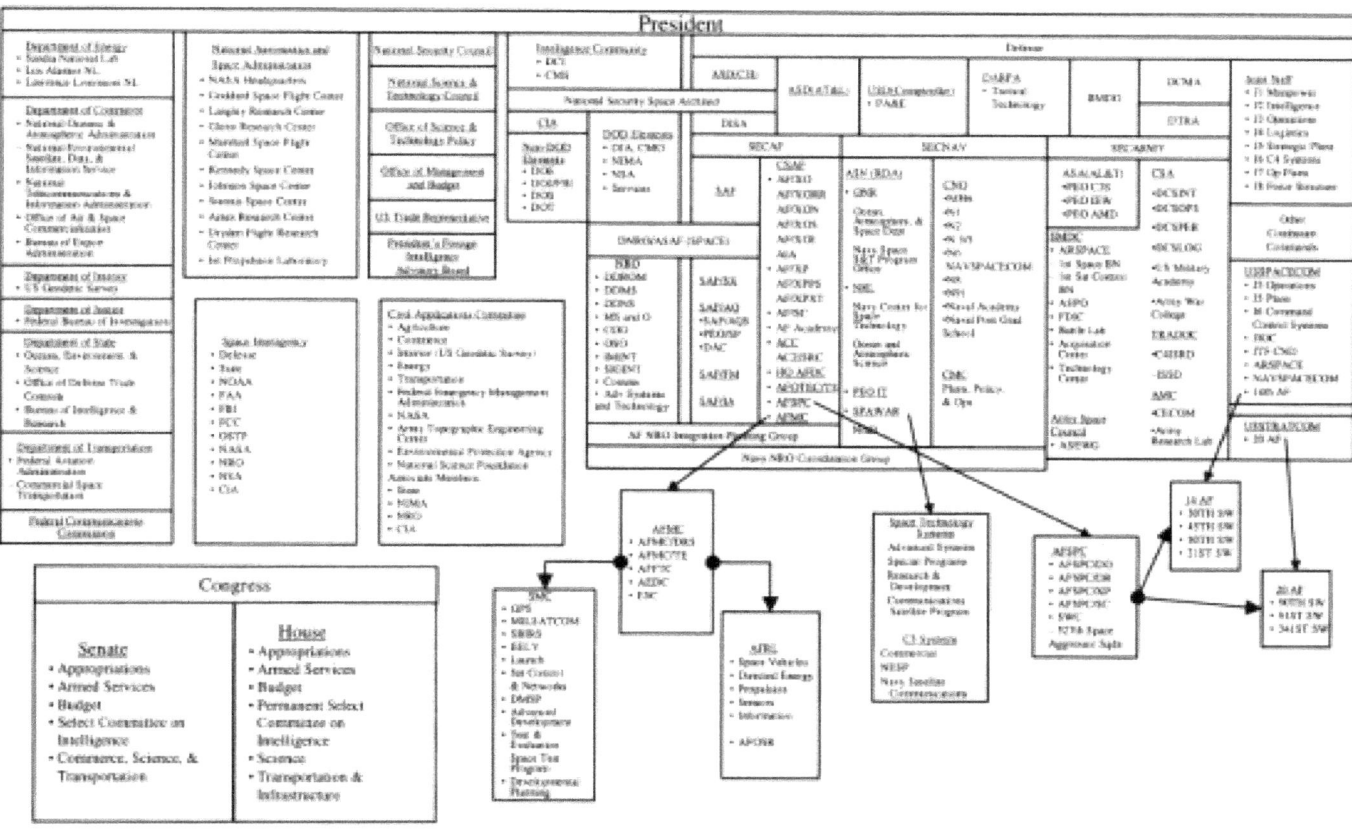

and Intelligence Community space activities. However, the assessment included consideration of civil and commercial activities to assess their relationship to and effect on national security space.

The Commission examined the role of organization and management in developing and implementing national-level guidance and in establishing requirements, acquiring and operating systems, and planning, programming and budgeting for national security space capabilities. The review concentrated on intelligence and military space operations as they relate to the needs of the national leadership as well as the needs of the military in conducting air, land and sea operations and independent space operations.

The Commission's unanimous findings and conclusions reflect its conviction that the U.S. has an urgent interest in promoting and protecting the peaceful use of space and in developing the technologies and operational capabilities that its objectives in space will require. This will require a focus on the long-term goals of national security space activities in the context of a dynamic and evolving security environment. Precisely because organizations need to adapt to changing events, the Commission focused its recommendations on near- and mid-term actions. The Commission believes these actions will better position U.S. space organizations and provide the direction and flexibility the U.S. needs to realize its longer-term interests in space. However, while organization and management are important, the critical need is national leadership to elevate space on the national security agenda.

> *While organization and management are important, the critical need is national leadership to elevate space on the national security agenda.*

The Commission reviewed a large number of studies completed over the last decade on the state of the nation's launch capabilities and facilities. The Commission is in broad agreement with these studies on the nation's clear needs in this area, particularly modernization of the launch infrastructure and vehicles.

Although the Commission was not asked to evaluate specific space programs, it did consider the Future Imagery Architecture (FIA), Space-Based Infrared System-Low (SBIRS-Low) and Discoverer-II programs as examples of the ways in which organizational and management interests can affect decisions on national security space programs.

The Commission's Charter

In evaluating alternative approaches to organizing and managing national security space activities, the Commission did not conduct a cost assessment of each approach. Instead, the advantages and disadvantages of organizational change were considered more broadly in terms of the opportunity costs of the status quo versus the advantages of making changes to better attain U.S. interests in space.

The Commission met with senior officials in the Department of Defense, including the Secretary of Defense, the Deputy Secretary of Defense and the Assistant Secretary of Defense for Command, Control, Communications and Intelligence (ASD(C3I)). It met with senior military leaders, including the Vice Chairman, Joint Chiefs of Staff, the Chief of Staff of the Air Force and, in a three-day session in Colorado Springs, Colorado, the military Commanders in Chief (CINCs) or their designated representatives. The Commission met with the Director of Central Intelligence, the Deputy Director of Central Intelligence for Community Management and the Directors of the National Security Agency (NSA), National Reconnaissance Office (NRO), and National Imagery and Mapping Agency (NIMA). The Commission met as well with the Administrator of the National Aeronautics and Space Administration (NASA).

The Commission had access to information from experts associated with the commercial, civil, defense and intelligence space sectors. To gain perspective for its analysis, the Commission met with former senior government officials. It met as well with the Chairmen of the National Commission for the Review of the National Reconnaissance Office and the Chairman of the Commission to Review the National Imagery and Mapping Agency. The Department of Defense and National Reconnaissance Office provided the Commissioners access to a number of classified space programs.

C. Organization of the Report

The report provides the Commission's views on:

- The role for space in future national security affairs and the challenges the U.S. is likely to confront to its commercial, civil, defense and intelligence interests in space.

- Objectives for advancing U.S. interests in space by enabling and encouraging development of policies, personnel, technologies and operations essential to maintaining U.S. leadership.

- U.S. agencies involved in national security space as a basis for understanding current practices and identifying alternative approaches to organization and management.

- Current management of space activity at the national level, within the Department of Defense and within the Intelligence Community.

- Recommendations for organization and management, including specific proposals to address discrete issues and problems identified in the course of the Commission's deliberations.

II. Space: Today and the Future

The security and economic well being of the United States and its allies and friends depend on the nation's ability to operate successfully in space. To be able to contribute to peace and stability in a distinctly different but still dangerous and complex global environment, the U.S. needs to remain at the forefront in space, technologically and operationally, as we have in the air, on land and at sea. Specifically, the U.S. must have the capability to use space as an integral part of its ability to manage crises, deter conflicts and, if deterrence fails, to prevail in conflict.

With the dramatic and still accelerating advances in science and technology, the use of space is increasing rapidly. Yet, the uses and benefits of space often go unrecognized. We live in an information age, driven by needs for precision, accuracy and timeliness in all of our endeavors—personal, business and governmental. As society becomes increasingly mobile and global, reliance on the worldwide availability of information will increase. Space-based systems, transmitting data, voice and video, will continue to play a critical part in collecting and distributing information. Space is also a medium in which highly valuable applications are being developed and around which highly lucrative economic endeavors are being built.

A. A New Era of Space

The first era of the space age was one of experimentation and discovery. Telstar, Mercury and Apollo, Voyager and Hubble, and the Space Shuttle taught Americans how to journey into space and allowed them to take the first tentative steps toward operating in space while enlarging their knowledge of the universe (Figure 4). While these programs were underway, the U.S. defense and intelligence communities were building and using satellites to conduct reconnaissance, warn of missile launches, chart the weather and allow commanders to

Source: Jeff Hester and Paul Scowen (Arizona State University) and NASA
Figure 4: Hubble space telescope image of the Eagle Nebula, 7,000 light years from the Earth

Space: Today and the Future

> *We are now on the threshold of a new era of the space age, devoted to mastering operations in space.*

communicate with their forces and to precisely locate objects in time and space. These programs were driven by the urgent need for information about threats to vital interests of the United States. During this era, the commercial space industry matured gradually as it learned to develop reliable communications satellites to carry voice, data and video over continents and oceans.

We are now on the threshold of a new era of the space age, devoted to mastering operations in space.

1. The Role for Space

There are four sectors of space activity: civil, commercial, defense and intelligence.

Civil Space Sector

The civil space sector is approaching a long-standing goal of a permanent manned presence in space with the deployment of astronauts to the International Space Station. The U.S. has shouldered the largest share of development and funding for this effort. Because it is an international program, however, its benefits for scientific research, experimentation and commercial processes will be widely shared. The number of countries able to participate in manned space flight has grown substantially. In addition to the U.S. and the USSR (now the Russian Federation), 21 other countries have sent astronauts into orbit in U.S. and Russian spacecraft. The People's Republic of China has announced its intention to become the third nation to place human beings in orbit and return them safely to earth.

Other research and experiments in the civil sector have many applications to human activity. For example, civil space missions to understand the effects of the sun on the earth, other planets and the space between them, such as those conducted by the Solar Terrestrial Probe missions, will help in the development of more advanced means to predict weather on earth.

> *The growth of the space industry today, and its hallmark in the future, will be space-based services.*

Commercial Space Sector

Unlike the earlier space era, in which governments drove activity in space, in this new era certain space applications, such as communications, are being driven by the commercial sector (Figure 5). An international space industry has developed, with revenues exceeding $80 billion in 2000. Industry forecasts project revenues will more than triple in the next decade. Whereas satellite system manufacturing once defined the market, the growth of the space industry today, and its hallmark in the future, will be space-based services.

Source: United States Coast Guard
Figure 5: Coast Guard rescue of the crew aboard the cruise ship Sea Breeze I relied on space-based communications and navigation

The space industry is marked by stiff competition among commercial firms to secure orbital locations for satellites and to secure the use of radio frequencies to exploit a global market for goods and services provided by those satellites. International consortia are pursuing many space enterprises, so ascertaining the national identity of a firm is increasingly complex. The calculations of financial investors in the industry and consumer buying habits are dominated by time to market, cost and price, quantity and quality. It is a volatile market. Nevertheless, as a result of the competition in goods and services, new applications for space-based systems continue to be developed, the use of those products is increasing and their market value is growing.

Space-based technology is revolutionizing major aspects of commercial and social activity and will continue to do so as the capacity and capabilities of satellites increase through emerging technologies. Space enters homes, businesses, schools, hospitals and government offices through its applications for transportation, health, the environment, telecommunications, education, commerce, agriculture and energy (Figure 6). Space-based technologies and services permit people to communicate, companies to do business, civic groups to serve the public and

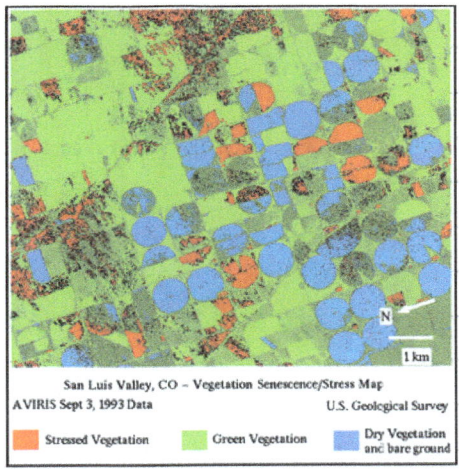

Source: USGS Spectroscopy Laboratory
Figure 6: Revolutionary satellite imaging products, simulated by this false color image, will enable new farming methods

Space: Today and the Future

> *The commercial revolution in space has eliminated the exclusive control of space once enjoyed by national defense, intelligence and government agencies.*

scientists to conduct research. Much like highways and airways, water lines and electric grids, services supplied from space are already an important part of the U.S. and global infrastructures.

The most telling feature of the new space age is that the commercial revolution in space has eliminated the exclusive control of space once enjoyed by national defense, intelligence and government agencies. For only a few thousand dollars, a customer today can purchase a photograph of an area on earth equal in quality to those formerly available only to the superpowers during the Cold War. Commercial providers can complement the photographic images with data that identify the location and type of foliage in an area and provide evidence of recent activity there. They can produce radar-generated maps with terrain elevations, transmit this information around the globe and combine all of it into formats most useful to the customer (Figure 7). This service is of increasing value to farmers and ranchers, fisherman and miners, city planners and scientists.

Source" Jet Propulsion Laboratory Planetary Photo Journal
Figure 7: Radar satellite imagery can detail natural phenomena in three dimensions, such as the eruption of this Japanese volcano on the populated island of Miyake-Jima.

Defense Space Sector

Space-related capabilities help national leaders to implement American foreign policy and, when necessary, to use military power in ways never before possible. Today, information gathered from and transmitted through space is an integral component of American military strategy and operations. Space-based capabilities enable military forces to be warned of missile attacks, to communicate instantaneously, to obtain near real-time information that can be transmitted rapidly from satellite to attack platform, to navigate to a conflict area while avoiding hostile defenses along the way, and to identify and strike targets from air, land or sea with precise and devastating effect. This permits U.S. leaders to manage even distant crises with fewer forces because those forces can respond quickly and operate effectively over longer ranges. Because of space capabilities, the U.S. is better able to sustain and extend deterrence to its allies and friends in our highly complex international environment.

Space is not simply a place from which information is acquired and transmitted or through which objects pass. It is a medium much the same as air, land or sea. In the coming period, the U.S. will conduct operations to, from, in and through space in support of its national interests both on earth and in space (Figure 8). As with national capabilities in the air, on land and at sea, the U.S. must have the capabilities to defend its space assets against hostile acts and to negate the hostile use of space against U.S. interests.

> *Space is a medium much the same as air, land or sea.*

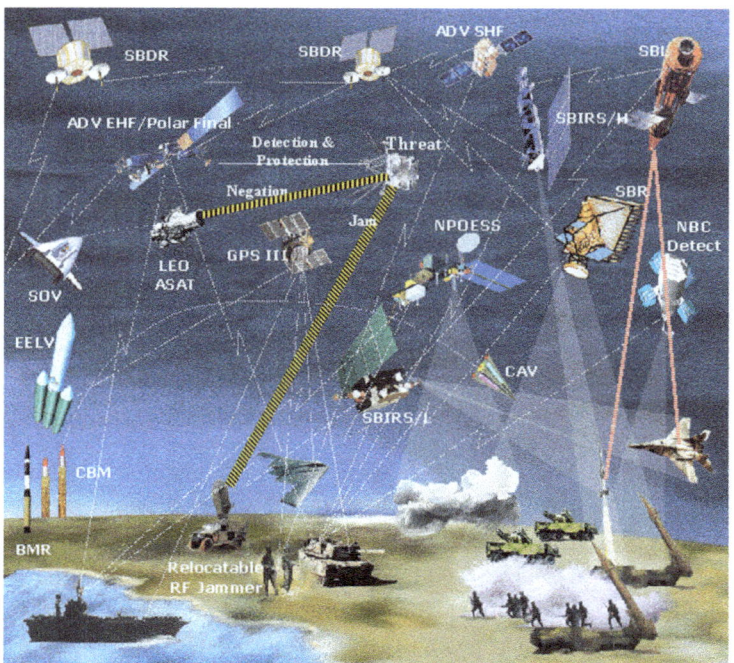

Source: Headquarters Air Force Space Command
Figure 8: Space systems will transform the conduct of future military operations

Space: Today and the Future

Intelligence Space Sector

Intelligence collected from space remains essential to the mission of the Intelligence Community, as it has been since the early 1960s. Then the need to gain access to a hostile, denied area, the USSR, drove the development of space-based intelligence collection. The need for access to denied areas persists. In addition, the U.S. Intelligence Community is required to collect information on a wide variety of subjects in support of U.S. global security policy.

> *Today, the U.S. Intelligence Community is required to collect information about many nations, organizations and even individuals.*

The Intelligence Community and the Department of Defense deploy satellites to provide global communications capabilities; verify treaties through "national technical means"; conduct photoreconnaissance; collect mapping, charting, geodetic, scientific and environmental data; and gather information on natural or man-made disasters (Figure 9). The U.S. also collects signals intelligence and measurement and signature intelligence from space. This intelligence is essential to the formulation of foreign and defense policies, the capacity of the President to manage crises and conflicts, the conduct of military operations and the development of military capabilities to assure the attainment of U.S. objectives.

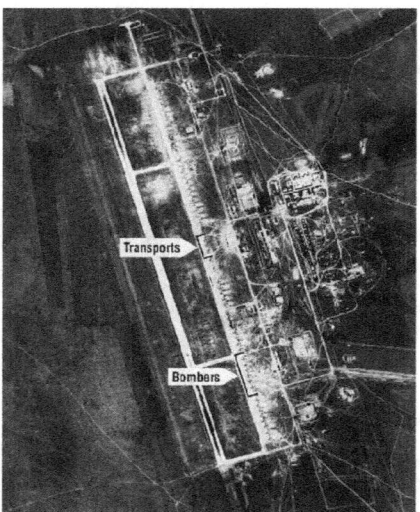

Source: National Reconnaissance Office, Corona Image of Dolon Airfield
Figure 9: Space-based image of a military airfield in the former USSR.

Modernizing the National Security Space Sector
The defense and intelligence space activities together comprise the national security space sector. The Department of Defense and the Intelligence Community are undertaking substantial and expensive programs to replace virtually their entire inventory of satellites and launch vehicles over the next decade or so. These programs are estimated to cost more than $60 billion during this period (Figure 10). Following are examples of space programs undergoing modernization:

- Intelligence collection systems designed in the late 1970s and early 1980s are scheduled for replacement in the near future. There are plans to improve the process for moving intelligence collected from these satellites to the users, both political and military.

- The military will deploy the next generation Global Positioning System (GPS), which will provide both military and civilian users with position, location and navigation with greater precision and reliability while improving the value of the system for military operations.

- Weather satellites operated by DoD are to be merged in a program jointly conducted with the National Oceanic and Atmospheric Administration (NOAA) and NASA, which will improve weather and environmental monitoring.

- To meet the military's growing reliance on information, all military communication satellites are planned to be replaced with more capable systems.

- Deployment of the Space-Based Infrared System (SBIRS) will improve the ability to detect ballistic missile launches. SBIRS will also provide significant contributions to missile defense and intelligence missions.

- The Space Based Laser program plans to demonstrate the technology to destroy a ballistic missile from space.

Space: Today and the Future

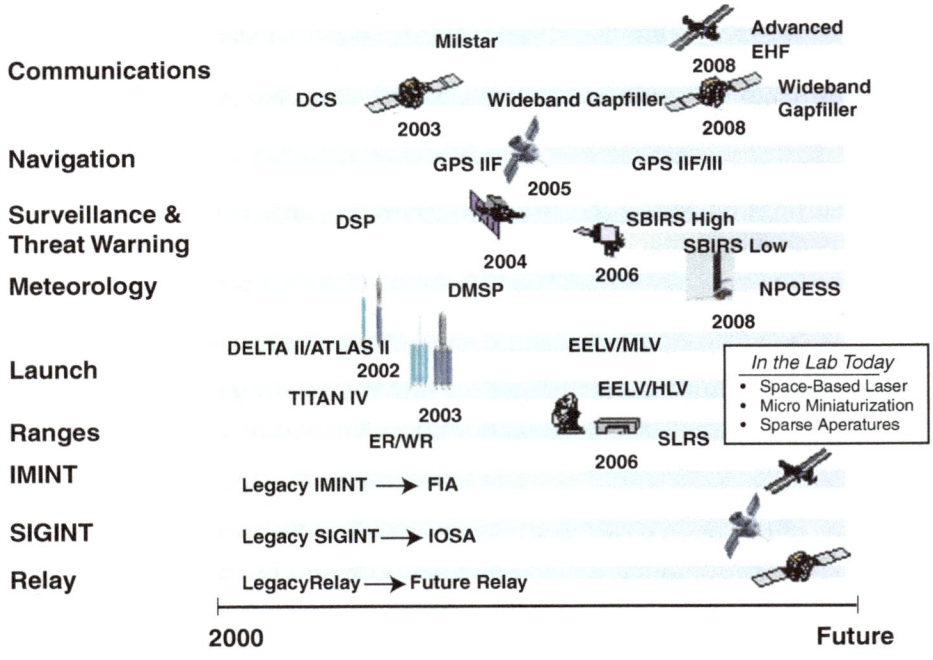

Source: Headquarters Air Force and National Reconnaissance Office

Figure 10: An extensive modernization program is underway for national security space systems

International Dimension

Opportunities in space are not limited to the United States. Many countries either conduct or participate in space programs dedicated to a variety of tasks, including communications and remote sensing. Although no country has a comprehensive space program to rival that of the United States, a growing number of nations have more limited programs or take part in international collaborative efforts in order to improve their own national security, commercial and civil space capabilities. Collaborative efforts are making space knowledge, technology, capabilities and applications increasingly available worldwide.

The U.S. will be tested over time by competing programs or attempts to restrict U.S. space activities through international regulations. In some countries such as Russia, China and India, "commercial" space programs are operated and controlled by the government, not private industry. In others, Israel, France and Japan, for example, the government has a strong influence over space companies, but these countries have a commercial space industry as well. Public and private entities in these and other countries are becoming competitive in the international market.

2. Toward the Future

Mastering near-earth space operations is still in its early stages. As mastery over operating in space is achieved, the value of activity in space will grow. Commercial space activity will become increasingly important to the global economy. Civil activity will involve more nations, international consortia and non-state actors. U.S. defense and intelligence activities in space will become increasingly important to the pursuit of U.S. national security interests.

The Commissioners appreciate the sensitivity that surrounds the notion of weapons in space for offensive or defensive purposes. They also believe, however, that to ignore the issue would be a disservice to the nation. The Commissioners believe the U.S. Government should vigorously pursue the capabilities called for in the National Space Policy to ensure that the President will have the option to deploy weapons in space to deter threats to and, if necessary, defend against attacks on U.S. interests.

B. Vulnerabilities and Threats

Space systems can be vulnerable to a range of attacks. These include disruption activities that temporarily deny access to space-derived products; activities that completely destroy a satellite system—the ground stations, launch systems or satellites on orbit; and those with the potential to render space useless for human purposes over an extended period of time. Launch systems are fragile. A launch failure can stop the U.S. from employing entire classes of boosters for extended periods of time. For example, after successive Titan failures in 1985 and 1986 and the Challenger Space Shuttle disaster in 1986, the nation experienced a 21-month hiatus in its ability to launch heavy national security payloads.

The political, economic and military value of space systems makes them attractive targets for state and non-state actors hostile to the United States and its interests. In order to extend its deterrence concepts and defense capabilities to space, the U.S. will require development of new military capabilities for operation to, from, in and through space. It will require, as well, engaging U.S. allies and friends, and the international community, in a sustained effort to fashion appropriate "rules of the road" for space.

1. Assessing the Threat Environment

The U.S. is more dependent on space than any other nation. Yet, the threat to the U.S. and its allies in and from space does not command the attention it merits from the departments and agencies of the U.S. Government charged with national security responsibilities. Consequently, evaluation of the threat to U.S. space capabilities currently lacks priority in the competition for collection and analytic resources.

> *The U.S. is more dependent on space than any other nation.*

The Intelligence Community has begun to improve its collection strategy for threats in and from space. Its analytic efforts, however, need to give more attention to the technical and operational forms a threat might take. The Intelligence Community needs to account fully for the implications of technology proliferation and services available on the open market to those entities that could threaten U.S. space capabilities. Political and military leaders need to appreciate the nature of the threat and should seek and receive from the Intelligence Community the necessary information on the space-related threat.

Failure to develop credible threat analyses could have serious consequences for the United States. It could leave the U.S. vulnerable to surprises in space and could result in deferred decisions on developing space-based capabilities due to the lack of a validated, well-understood threat. Surprise, however, is not limited to the possibility of an attack on U.S. systems. The U.S. also could be surprised by the emergence of new technological capabilities in the hands of potential adversaries. Or, the U.S. could be surprised in the international arena by economic or arms control proposals it does not anticipate, or the importance of which it does not fully appreciate, because of insufficient knowledge about the technical or operational capabilities of current or future negotiating partners.

2. Existing and Emerging Threats

The ability to restrict or deny freedom of access to and operations in space is no longer limited to global military powers. Knowledge of space systems and the means to counter them is increasingly available on the international market. Nations hostile to the U.S. possess or can acquire the means to disrupt or destroy U.S. space systems by attacking the satellites in space, their communications nodes on the ground and in space, or ground nodes that command the satellites.

Small nations, groups or even individuals can acquire from commercial sources imagery of targets on earth and in space. They can acquire accurate timing and navigational data and critical weather information generated by government-owned satellites. Improved command and control capabilities are available through the use of commercial communications satellites. Even launch capabilities can be contracted for with legitimate companies, and a number of smaller nations are developing their own space launch vehicles. The reality is that there are many extant capabilities, such as those described below, to deny, disrupt or physically destroy space systems and the ground facilities that use and control them.

Attacking Ground Stations
One of the more accessible ways to disrupt space systems is by attacking the associated satellite ground stations. This can be accomplished by a variety of means, ranging from physical attack to computer network intrusion.

Denial and Deception
Countries can attempt to defeat the reconnaissance function of satellites by obtaining sufficient information about the satellites' orbital and sensor characteristics. This information can be used to either deny access to the reconnaissance targets at critical times or to carry out deception efforts to confuse and complicate their signatures. As more information is made available concerning reconnaissance satellite characteristics, denial and deception are made easier and information collection more difficult.

Jamming Satellites on Orbit
Commercial satellite ground communications equipment has electronic jamming capabilities that can easily be used to disrupt the functions of some satellites. Many countries also have military jamming capabilities, including Russia and China as well as Iran, Cuba, Iraq and North Korea. Most U.S. commercial and civil satellites lack built-in protection measures

and are vulnerable to such attacks. Recent examples of satellite jamming include Indonesia jamming a transponder on a Chinese-owned satellite and Iran and Turkey jamming satellite TV broadcasts of dissidents. More sophisticated technologies for jamming satellite signals are becoming available. For example, Russia is marketing a handheld GPS jamming system (Figure 11). A one-watt version of that system, the size of a cigarette pack, is able to deny access to GPS out to 80 kilometers; a slightly larger version can deny access out to 192 kilometers. Both are compact and powerful enough to jam an aircraft's GPS receiver signal, which could disrupt military missions or create havoc at a civilian airport.

Source: National Air Intelligence Center
Figure 11: Russian handheld GPS jammers are available commercially worldwide.

Microsatellites

Advances in miniaturization and the proliferation of space technologies create opportunities for many countries to enter space with small, lightweight, inexpensive and highly capable systems that can perform a variety of missions (Figure 12). Microsatellites and nanosatellites, weighing from 100 kilograms to 10 kilograms, respectively, are examples of the advances in miniaturized space system technologies. Microsatellites can perform satellite inspection, imaging and other functions and could be adapted as weapons. Placed on an interception course and programmed to home on a satellite, a microsatellite could fly alongside a target until commanded to disrupt, disable or destroy the target. Detection of and defense against such an attack could prove difficult.

Space: Today and the Future

Source: National Air Intelligence Center
Figure 12: Many countries use microsatellites today for missions such as on-orbit inspection and remote sensing.

Technology transfer programs exist to train nations in the development and deployment of microsatellite systems. Commercial entities offer to teach customers how to design, develop, launch and operate small satellites, some as small as a portable compact disc player. Services have been provided to France, the United Kingdom and the United States, and technology transfer programs have been conducted with China, South Korea, Portugal, Pakistan, Chile, South Africa, Thailand, Singapore, Turkey and Malaysia. Companies in the United States and the United Kingdom, as well as other countries including Russia, Israel, Canada and Sweden, are involved in maturing microsatellite technology.

Nuclear Detonation

Perhaps the most devastating threat could come from a low-yield nuclear device, on the order of 50 kilotons, detonated a few hundred kilometers above the atmosphere. A nuclear detonation would increase ambient radiation to a level sufficient to severely damage nearby satellites and reduce the lifetime of satellites in low earth orbit from years to months or less. The lingering effects of radiation could make satellite operations futile for many

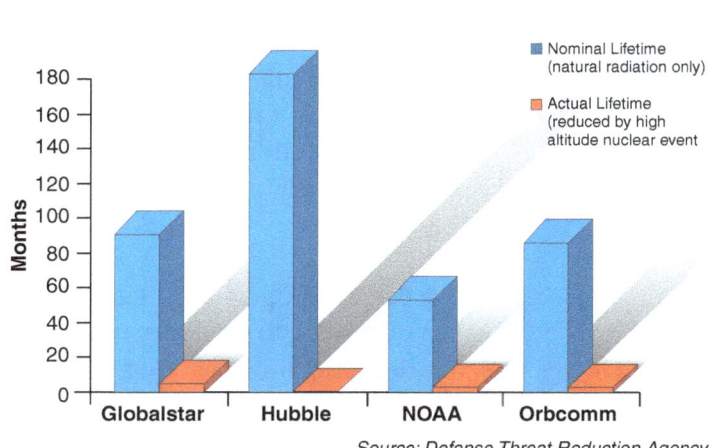

Source: Defense Threat Reduction Agency
Figure 13: Impact of a nuclear detonation on the lifetime of satellites

months. Even nuclear detonations in the 10-kiloton range could have significant effects on satellites for many months (Figure 13). To execute this mission, all that is needed is a rocket and a simple nuclear device. Countries such as Iran, North Korea, Iraq and Pakistan possess missiles that could carry warheads to the necessary altitudes and either have, or are believed to be developing, nuclear weapons.

3. Reducing Vulnerability

As harmful as the loss of commercial satellites or damage to civil assets would be, an attack on intelligence and military satellites would be even more serious for the nation in time of crisis or conflict. The U.S. could be subjected to serious difficulties if the functions of U.S. satellites were significantly disrupted or degraded as the President was working to ease a crisis between nuclear-armed adversaries or to end a conflict before an adversary used weapons of mass destruction against the U.S. or its allies.

The U.S. is an attractive candidate for a "Space Pearl Harbor."

As history has shown—whether at Pearl Harbor, the killing of 241 U.S. Marines in their barracks in Lebanon or the attack on the USS Cole in Yemen—if the U.S. offers an inviting target, it may well pay the price of attack. With the growing commercial and national security use of space, U.S. assets in space and on the ground offer just such targets. The U.S. is an attractive candidate for a "Space Pearl Harbor." The warning signs of U.S. vulnerability include:

- In 1998, the Galaxy IV satellite malfunctioned, shutting down 80 percent of U.S. pagers, as well as video feeds for cable and broadcast transmission, credit card authorization networks and corporate communications systems (Figure 14). To restore satellite service, satellites had to be moved and thousands of ground antennas had to be manually repositioned, which took weeks in some cases.

- In early 2000, the U.S. lost all information from a number of its satellites for three hours when computers in ground stations malfunctioned.

- In July 2000, the Xinhau news agency reported that China's military is developing methods and strategies for defeating the U.S. military in a high-tech and space-based future war. It noted, "for countries that could never win a war by using the method of tanks and planes, attacking the U.S. space system may be an irresistible and most tempting choice. . ." These reports illustrate a troubling but little-noticed view of the future.

- Hackers are routinely probing DoD networks and computers. The U.S. Space Command's Joint Task Force for Computer Network Defense reported that detected probes and scans are increasing, access to hacking tools is becoming easier and hacking techniques are becoming more sophisticated. In 1999 the number of detected probes and scans against DoD systems was just over 22,000; in the first eleven months of 2000, the number had grown to 26,500.

Source: Boeing Space and Communications
Figure 14: Malfunction of the Galaxy IV satellite shut down 80% of the nation's pagers

- If the GPS system were to experience widespread failure or disruption, the impact could be serious. Loss of GPS timing could disable police, fire and ambulance communications around the world; disrupt the global banking and financial system, which depends on GPS timing to keep worldwide financial centers connected; and interrupt the operation of electric power distribution systems.

The signs of vulnerability are not always so clear as those described above and therefore are not always recognized. Hostile actions against space systems can reasonably be confused with natural phenomena. Space debris or solar activity can "explain" the loss of a space system and mask unfriendly actions or the potential thereof. They can be explained as computer hardware or software failure, even though either might be the result of malicious acts. Thus far, the indicators have been neither sufficiently persuasive nor gripping to energize the U.S. to take appropriate defensive steps. For this reason, the Commission believes that the U.S. is not as yet well prepared to handle the range of potential threats to its space systems.

Threats to U.S. space systems might arise under a variety of conditions:

- In peacetime, as a terrorist act.

- In time of crisis, as an act of coercion or escalation.

- In wartime, as an effort to degrade U.S. intelligence or military performance.

Threatening or attacking the space capabilities of the U.S. would have domestic, economic and political consequences and could provoke international disputes about the origin and intent of an attack. Such ambiguity and uncertainty could be fatal to the successful management of a crisis or resolution of a conflict. They could lead to forbearance when action is needed or to hasty action when more or better information would have given rise to a broader and more effective set of response options.

There are a number of possible crises or conflicts in which the potential vulnerability of national security space systems would be worrisome. For example:

- Efforts to identify and strike terrorist strongholds and facilities in advance of or in retaliation for terrorist attacks on U.S. forces or citizens abroad, or on the U.S. homeland or that of its allies.

- Conflict in the Taiwan Straits, in which the U.S. attempts to deter escalation through the conduct of military operations while seeking to bring it to a favorable end through diplomatic measures.

- War in the Middle East, posing a threat to U.S. friends and allies in the region and calling for a rapid political and military response to threats by an aggressor to launch ballistic missiles armed with weapons of mass destruction.

- The disabling of a remote sensing satellite being used by a regional power to monitor Southwest Asia, followed shortly thereafter by another state in the region launching a long range ballistic missile armed with a weapon of mass destruction.

- Cyber attacks on nuclear command and control systems that precipitate a crisis in South Asia involving India and Pakistan and their respective allies.

In each of these contingencies and others like them, the President, his senior advisors and military commanders would be dependent on U.S. satellite systems to help manage the crisis, conduct military operations or bring about a resolution to the conflict. If the performance of U.S. systems were affected, the diplomatic and military leverage of the U.S. could be reduced, that of an adversary improved, and the cost and risks associated with achieving U.S. objectives commensurately increased.

That U.S. space systems might be threatened or attacked in such contingencies may seem improbable, even reckless. However, as political economist Thomas Schelling has pointed out, "There is a tendency in our planning to confuse the unfamiliar with the improbable. The contingency we have not considered looks strange; what looks strange is thought improbable; what is improbable need not be considered seriously." Surprise is most often not a lack of warning, but the result of a tendency to dismiss as reckless what we consider improbable.

History is replete with instances in which warning signs were ignored and change resisted until an external, "improbable" event forced resistant bureaucracies to take action. The question is whether the U.S. will be wise enough to act responsibly and soon enough to reduce U.S. space vulnerability. Or whether, as in the past, a disabling attack against the country and its people—a "Space Pearl Harbor"—will be the only event able to galvanize the nation and cause the U.S. Government to act.

> *We are on notice, but we have not noticed.*

We are on notice, but we have not noticed.

III. U.S. Objectives for Space

How the U.S. develops the potential of space for civil, commercial, defense and intelligence purposes will affect the nation's security for decades to come.

America's interests in space are to:

- Promote the peaceful use of space.

- Use the nation's potential in space to support U.S. domestic, economic, diplomatic and national security objectives.

- Develop and deploy the means to deter and defend against hostile acts directed at U.S. space assets and against the uses of space hostile to U.S. interests.

> *How the U.S. develops the potential of space for civil, commercial, defense and intelligence purposes will affect the nation's security for decades to come.*

The U.S. Government must work actively to make sure that the nation has the means necessary to advance its interests in space. To do so, it must direct its activities to:

- Transform U.S. military capabilities.

- Strengthen U.S. intelligence capabilities.

- Shape the international legal and regulatory environment that affects activities in space.

- Advance U.S. technological leadership related to space operations.

- Create and sustain a cadre of space professionals.

Concerted efforts in these areas are needed to enhance the nation's security by improving its capacity to deter aggression, to defend its interests and to pursue its civil space programs with modern and more capable systems. Deliberate, coherent policies in these areas also provide incentives to the commercial sector to pursue new activities in space and to develop new applications for goods and services derived from space systems. This essential combination of both government and private activity will be needed to keep the U.S. the world's leading space-faring nation.

A. Transform U.S. Military Capabilities

The United States must develop, deploy and maintain the means to deter attack on and to defend vulnerable space capabilities. Explicit national security guidance and defense policy is needed to direct development of doctrine, concepts of operations and capabilities for space, including weapons systems that operate in space and that can defend assets in orbit and augment air, land and sea forces. This requires a deterrence strategy for space, which in turn must be supported by a broader range of space capabilities.

A deterrence strategy for space...must be supported by a greater range of space capabilities.

1. Deterrence and Defense Policy for Space

The 1996 National Space Policy states, "Purposeful interference with space systems shall be viewed as an infringement on sovereign rights." That policy directs that steps be taken to protect against attack through such measures as deploying sensors on satellites, hardening them to electromagnetic effects and radiation and improving the security of ground stations and communication links. It also directs that measures be taken to prevent attack on the communication links by encrypting messages, by tracking satellites and through warnings. Generally, commercial satellite operators have not seen a need to do this, as there are associated costs and customers have not demanded protection measures.

Current policy also calls for a capability to negate threats to the use of space by the United States. In 1999 then-Deputy Secretary of Defense John Hamre stated that the preferred U.S. approach was "tactical denial of capabilities" used by an adversary, not "permanent destruction." The U.S. "reserves the right to be able to retaliate and destroy" either ground sites or satellites, if necessary. The preferred approach to negation is the use of effects that are "temporary and reversible in their nature."

Such approaches rely on jamming signals or interfering with the function of hostile satellites rather than disabling or destroying them. Temporary and reversible approaches are technically elegant and valuable, but they may not serve equally well across the full spectrum of possible contingencies. This is especially true when it is important to know with high confidence that a satellite can no longer function.

The U.S. will require means of negating satellite threats, whether temporary and reversible or physically destructive. The senior political and military leadership needs to test these capabilities in exercises on a regular basis, both to keep the armed forces proficient in their use and to bolster their deterrent effect on potential adversaries. Besides computer-based simulations and other wargaming techniques, these exercises should include "live fire" events. These "live fire" events will require the development of testing ranges in space and procedures for their use that protect the on-orbit assets of the U.S. and other space-faring nations. While exercises may give adversaries information they can use to challenge U.S. space capabilities, that risk must be balanced against the fact that capabilities that are untested, unknown or unproven cannot be expected to deter.

A policy of deterrence would need to be extended to U.S. allies and friends, consistent with U.S. treaty obligations and U.S. interests. In the case of NATO, the U.S. might consider whether a planning group should be formed to develop a common appreciation of the threats, discuss potential responses and consult on the formulation of alliance policy and plans to deter and defend against threats from space. Only by extensive prior consultation, planning and appropriate exercises will the U.S. have the cooperation it would need in a crisis.

2. Assured Access to Space and On-Orbit Operations

United States deterrence and defense capabilities depend critically on assured and timely access to space. The U.S. should continue to pursue revolutionary reusable launch vehicle technologies and systems even as the U.S. moves to the next generation of expendable launch vehicles (Figure 15). In addition, the U.S. must invest in technologies that will enable satellites to be operational shortly after launch. One key objective of these technological advances must be to reduce substantially the cost of

Source: United States Space Command
Figure 15: Reusable launch vehicles offer new approaches for operating to, from and in space.

placing objects and capabilities in orbit, while providing the means to launch operationally useful satellites, both on short notice and on routine schedules.

If the U.S. is to master space operations, its launch capabilities must respond both to national security needs and to commercial and civil sector requirements. This calls for a modern launch infrastructure and modern launch vehicles. Today's U.S. launch infrastructure, which includes launch complexes, processing facilities and tracking systems, needs modernization. The nation lacks an overall vision for launch that accommodates the evolving and essential partnership between the government and commercial industry.

> *One key objective of these technological advances must be to substantially reduce the cost of placing objects and capabilities in orbit.*

The ranges and their associated launch complexes, at Cape Canaveral AFB and Kennedy Space Flight Center on the east coast and Vandenberg AFB on the west coast, have enough capacity to meet the projected needs of all users under normal conditions. However, more capacity is needed to provide for margin and flexibility to handle launch "surges," to accommodate launch delays and to allow launch areas to undergo scheduled maintenance and modernization. The U.S. should seek to streamline the processes associated with integrating spacecraft with launch vehicles. The U.S. also needs to implement plans to reduce range costs and improve flexibility by using more efficient technology, such as GPS and satellite-based communications, in the areas of range safety and tracking.

Along with assured access to space, the U.S. needs to develop better ways to conduct operations once in space. New approaches to on-orbit propulsion can improve spacecraft maneuverability and safety, and on-orbit servicing can extend the life of space systems and upgrade their capabilities after launch. Autonomous, reusable orbit transfer systems can provide greater maneuverability in and between different orbits. In addition, the Defense Advanced Research Projects Agency, the Air Force and NASA are studying robotic microsatellites that can provide spacecraft servicing. When coupled with spacecraft that allow for modular component replacement while on orbit, these systems could provide significant life cycle cost savings, and would enable spacecraft and interchangeable payloads to be upgraded.

3. Space Situational Awareness

To use space effectively and to protect against threats that may originate from it, the U.S. must be able to identify and track much smaller objects in space than it can track today (Figure 16). The current space surveillance network, the earth-based radars and cameras used to track objects in space, needs modernization and expansion. An improved space surveillance network is needed to reduce the chance of collision between satellites, the Space Shuttle or the International Space Station and the thousands of pieces of space debris orbiting the earth. It will also have to track objects deeper in space, such as asteroids or spacecraft. And to reduce the possibility of surprise by hostile actors, it will have to monitor space activity. The evolution of technology and the character of this problem argue for placing elements of the surveillance network in space, including both electro-optical and radar systems.

Source: National Aeronautics and Space Administration's Orbital Debris Program Office, Johnson Space Center

Figure 16: Space situational awareness requires tracking and identifying many thousands of objects in space, not only the satellites illustrated here.

4. Earth Surveillance From Space

Space provides a unique vantage point for observing objects across vast reaches of air, land and sea. The U.S. needs to develop technologies for sensors, communication, power generation and space platforms that will enable it to observe the earth and objects in motion on a near real-time basis, 24 hours-a-day. If deployed, these could revolutionize military operations. For example, a space-based radar, such as the recently cancelled Discoverer II program, could provide military commanders, on a near-continuous and global basis, with timely, precise information on the location of adversary forces and their movement over time. Coupled to precision strike weapons delivered rapidly over long distances, even conventionally armed inter-continental ballistic missiles, space-based radar surveillance would enhance deterrence of hostile action. The same space-based technologies could revolutionize public and private transportation, traffic management and disaster relief operations by providing information on the location, routing and status of vehicles.

5. Global Command, Control and Communications in Space

Development of a Global Information Grid—a globally interconnected, end-to-end set of information capabilities and associated processes that will allow the warfighter, policy makers and support personnel to access information on demand—will rely on space assets to provide the command, control and communications (C3) required by enroute, mobile and deployed military forces.

6. Defense in Space

Assuring the security of space capabilities becomes more challenging as technology proliferates and access to it by potentially hostile entities becomes easier. The loss of space systems that support military operations or collect intelligence would dramatically affect the way U.S. forces could fight, likely raising the cost in lives and property and making the outcome less sure. U.S. space systems, including the ground, communication and space segments, need to be defended to ensure their survivability.

Providing active and passive protection to assets that could be at risk during peacetime, crisis or conflict is increasingly urgent. New technologies for microsatellites, hardened electronics, autonomous operations and reusable launch vehicles are needed to improve the survivability of satellites on orbit as well as the ability to rapidly replace systems that have malfunctioned, been disabled or been destroyed.

7. Homeland Defense

Some believe the ballistic missile defense mission is best performed when both sensors and interceptors are deployed in space. Effective sensors make countermeasures more difficult, and interceptors make it possible to destroy a missile shortly after launch, before either warhead or countermeasures are released.

8. Power Projection In, From and Through Space

Finally, space offers advantages for basing systems intended to affect air, land and sea operations. Many think of space only as a place for passive collection of images or signals or a switchboard that can quickly pass information back and forth over long distances. It is also possible to project power through and from space in response to events anywhere in the world. Unlike weapons from aircraft, land forces or ships, space missions initiated from earth or space could be carried out with little transit, information or weather delay. Having this capability would give the U.S. a much stronger deterrent and, in a conflict, an extraordinary military advantage.

> *It is also possible to project power through and from space in response to events anywhere in the world.*

B. Strengthen Intelligence Capabilities

The U.S. needs to strengthen its ability to collect information about the activities, capabilities and intentions of potential adversaries and to overcome their efforts to deny the U.S. this information. Since the end of the Cold War, the number, complexity and scope of high-priority tasks assigned to the Intelligence Community have increased even as its human resources and technical advantage have eroded. This has reduced the Intelligence Community's ability to provide timely and accurate estimates of threats and has correspondingly increased the possibility of surprise.

1. Tasks of the Intelligence Community

The growth in collection requirements is a result of the broader nature of U.S. security interests in the decade since the end of the Cold War. Once concerned primarily with the Soviet Union, the Intelligence Community is now tasked to monitor political, economic and even environmental developments in many places around the globe. Tasking related to national security has expanded as well. The Intelligence Community is tasked to collect scientific, technical and military information on countries potentially hostile to the U.S. or its allies. It is tasked to collect intelligence to support anti-drug efforts and anti-terrorism operations, such as the pursuit of the terrorist Osama bin Laden. Amidst these tasks, the Community has as its highest priority support for forward-deployed military forces engaged in a variety of missions to include peace enforcement operations.

2. Revolutionary Collection Methods

With the growth and use of fiber optic cable and the employment of active denial and deception measures by potential adversaries, intelligence collection from space is increasingly difficult. Information published on the Internet or elsewhere, available through unauthorized disclosure or through espionage is used by adversaries to avoid and disrupt U.S. intelligence collection efforts. This, in turn, increases the time, effort and money needed to collect information and can reduce the value of the resulting intelligence product. Nevertheless, collection from space will continue to be critical to meeting difficult intelligence collection challenges.

To meet the challenges posed to space-based intelligence collection, the U.S. needs to review its approach to intelligence collection from space. Current strategy seeks to capitalize on known technologies to improve collection capabilities in ways that will provide intelligence users, especially military forces in the field, with information in a timely fashion.

While the current collection strategy has been a boon to military forces and crisis managers, planned and programmed collection platforms may not be adaptable enough to meet the many and varied tasks assigned. The U.S. must invest in space-based collection technologies that will provide revolutionary methods for collecting intelligence, especially on difficult intelligence targets. This is essential if the U.S. is to conduct complex diplomatic initiatives successfully, provide strategic warning of significant political and military events, support research into countermeasures to the weapons of potential adversaries, and maintain its other activities not directly related to military operations.

> ***The United States must invest in revolutionary space-based collection technologies.***

3. Leveraging Commercial Products

To the extent that commercial products, particularly imagery from U.S. commercial remote sensing companies, can meet intelligence collection needs, these should be incorporated into the overall collection architecture. Current policy endorses and encourages this use.

The reasons for the policy are clear and compelling. Commercial imagery providers are now licensed to provide half-meter imagery, a resolution that allows the human eye to see objects as small as an automobile or differentiate between classes of military vehicles (Figure 17). Informed estimates suggest that data of this resolution and quality would satisfy approximately half of NIMA's requirements for information on the location of objects on the earth.

In particular, commercial imagery systems could be used for wide-area surveillance, freeing government satellites for more challenging, point-target reconnaissance. More aggressive government use of commercial imagery would also help to solidify the position of American companies in a fiercely competitive international market. However, the government has neither established a systematic process for tasking, processing and disseminating commercial imagery, nor budgeted the resources to use commercial products to meet customer needs.

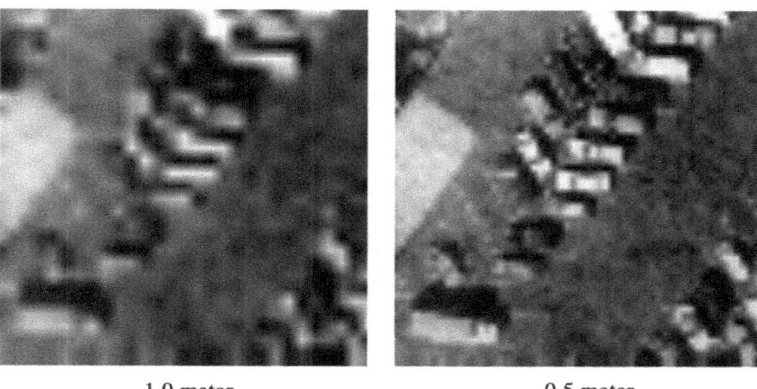

1.0 meter   0.5 meter

Source: Intelligence Resource Program of the Federation of American Scientists, http://www.fas.org/irp
Figure 17: The U.S. Government has recently approved the sale of half-meter commercial imagery

Freed from providing so-called "commodity products," the Intelligence Community would be able to concentrate on more innovative technologies and take greater risk in designing future systems to overcome the growing challenges to collection. This approach should include demonstration efforts that could provide the foundation for new approaches to collection.

In designing and funding both current and revolutionary collection systems, the Intelligence Community needs to take new initiatives and dedicate more resources to planning and funding its tasking, processing, exploitation and distribution system for intelligence. If not delivered in a timely way to the user, even the best information is worse than useless.

C. Shape the International Legal and Regulatory Environment

U.S. activity in space, both governmental and commercial, is governed by treaties and by international and domestic law and regulations, which have contributed to the orderly use of space by all nations. As interest in and use of space increases, both within the United States and around the world, the U.S. must participate actively in shaping the space legal and regulatory environment. Because of its investment in space and its increasing dependence on space-based capabilities, the U.S. has a large stake in how this environment evolves. To protect the country's interests, the U.S. must promote the peaceful use of space, monitor activities of regulatory bodies, and protect the rights of nations to defend their interests in and from space.

> *The U.S. must participate actively in shaping the space legal and regulatory environment.*

1. Impact on the Military Use of Space

International Law
A number of existing principles of international law apply to space activity. Chief among these are the definition of "peaceful purposes," the right of self-defense and the effect of hostilities on treaties. The U.S. and most other nations interpret "peaceful" to mean "non-aggressive"; this comports with customary international law allowing for routine military activities in outer space, as it does on the high seas and in international airspace.

U.S. Objectives for Space

There is no blanket prohibition in international law on placing or using weapons in space, applying force from space to earth or conducting military operations in and through space. There are a number of specific prohibitions on activity to which the U.S. has agreed:

- The 1963 Limited Test Ban Treaty prohibits "any nuclear weapon test explosion, or any other nuclear explosion" in outer space.

- The 1967 Outer Space Treaty proscribes placing weapons of mass destruction in space or on the moon or other celestial bodies, and using the moon or other celestial bodies for any military purposes.

- The 1972 Anti-Ballistic Missile (ABM) Treaty prohibits the development, testing, or deployment of space-based components of an anti-ballistic missile system.

- A number of arms control treaties are intended to prohibit the U.S and Russia from interfering with the other's use of satellites for monitoring treaty compliance.

- The 1980 Environmental Modification Convention prohibits all hostile actions that might cause long-lasting, severe or widespread environmental effects in space.

It is important to note, however, that by specifically extending the principles of the U.N. Charter to space, the Outer Space Treaty (Article III) provides for the right of individual and collective self-defense, including "anticipatory self-defense." In addition, the non-interference principle established by space law treaties would be suspended among belligerents during a state of hostilities.

Emerging Challenges

To counter U.S. advantages in space, other states and international organizations have sought agreements that would restrict the use of space. For example, nearly every year, the U.N. General Assembly passes a resolution calling for prevention of "an arms race in outer space" by prohibiting all space weapons. Russia and China have proposed to prohibit the use of space for national missile defense. The U.S. should seek to preserve the space weapons regime established by the Outer Space Treaty, particularly the traditional interpretation of the Treaty's "peaceful purposes" language to mean that both self-defense and non-aggressive military use of space are allowed.

The U.S. should review existing arms control obligations in light of a growing need to extend deterrent capabilities to space. These agreements were not meant to restrict lawful space activity outside the scope of each treaty. For example, ABM Treaty prohibitions on space-based ABM systems should not apply to other types of space-based systems that do not meet its definitions. Similarly, while international treaty law holds that arms control and other treaties may be suspended between belligerents during a state of conflict, the changing character of conflict requires careful consideration of U.S. obligations when the status of belligerents may be unclear.

> *The changing character of conflict requires careful consideration of U.S. obligations when the status of belligerents may be unclear.*

The U.S. must be cautious of agreements intended for one purpose that, when added to a larger web of treaties or regulations, may have the unintended consequence of restricting future activities in space. One recent example is the agreement signed between the U.S. and Russia on a Pre- and Post-Launch Notification System (PLNS), intended to minimize the consequences of a false missile attack warning. It requires at least 24-hour advance notice of every significant launch. The PLNS may establish a precedent for using international agreements to regulate space launch. Its specific provisions, which apply both to ballistic missiles and conventional space launch vehicles, could prove to be a significant burden if applied to systems now being designed to provide "better, faster, cheaper" access to space.

2. Satellite Regulation

U.S. satellite companies face many new legal and regulatory challenges. Traditional priorities and alliances are shifting, and international negotiations are becoming less predictable and more complex. Globalization is increasing. Foreign satellite services entering the U.S. market may bring competitive advantages to the United States and may also raise national security concerns. At the same time, more governments are expanding their use of satellite systems, raising critical near-term regulatory issues. For example:

- *Radio Frequency Spectrum.* Demands for radio frequency spectrum are escalating because of the pro-competitive market-opening effects of the 1997 World Trade Organization Agreement, as well as new and expanded uses of radio-frequency spectrum. As a result, the allocation, assignment and coordination of radio-frequency spectrum for government and non-government purposes is becoming more difficult and time-consuming. Nations and international organizations are addressing these issues, which have significant security and economic implications worldwide.

- ***Export Controls.*** Different arms of the U.S. Government have widely differing and sometimes contradictory perspectives toward exports. While export controls can prevent technology from falling into dangerous hands, a process that is too onerous and time-consuming can needlessly restrict U.S. companies in the international market, weaken the U.S. space industry in the global market and eventually erode U.S. technological leadership.

Looking toward the future, the U.S. challenge is to shape a domestic and international legal and regulatory framework that ensures U.S. national security and enhances the commercial and civil space sectors. This means strengthening and supporting the competitive position of U.S. interests in space commerce. An effective interagency process needs to be put in place to identify and address the multiple U.S. interests, sort out the implications of U.S. policies and positions and avoid uncoordinated decisions.

D. Advance U.S. Technological Leadership

To achieve national security objectives and compete successfully internationally, the U.S. must maintain technological leadership in space. This requires a healthy industrial base, inproved science and technology resources, an attitude of risk-taking and innovation, and government policies that support international competitiveness. In particular, the government needs to significantly increase its investment in breakthrough technologies to fuel innovative, revolutionary capabilities. Mastery of space also requires new approaches that reduce significantly the

> *The U.S. will not remain the world's leading spacefaring nation by relying on yesterday's technology to meet today's requirements at tomorrow's prices.*

cost of building and launching space systems. The U.S. will not remain the world's leading space-faring nation by relying on yesterday's technology to meet today's requirements at tomorrow's prices.

1. Investment in Research and Development

Research and development investment is a powerful engine to drive industrial growth. Aerospace research and development investments of the 1960s through the 1980s propelled the U.S. into world leadership in the space business. Since the 1980s, however, the aerospace sector's share of the total national research and development investment has decreased from nearly 20 percent to less than 8 percent, an amount insufficient to maintain the nation's leadership position in space in the coming decades.

The problem is compounded by how industry is investing its research and development resources. U.S. companies are investing most of the independent research and development funds available to help win modernization contracts rather than invest in "leap ahead" technologies.

2. Government/Industry Relationship

The U.S. Government needs to develop a new relationship with industry to ensure U.S. space technological leadership.

The recent *U.S. Space Industrial Base Study* that surveyed 21 major defense contractors found the space industry plagued by deteriorating financial health, a high debt burden, and a rate of return that is often less than the cost of raising funds. The government should be sensitive to this situation and ensure that its policies allow industry to realize a reasonable rate of return on its investment in the space business.

> *The U.S. Government needs to develop a new relationship with industry to ensure U.S. space technological leadership.*

To advance technological leadership, the goal is to ensure conditions exist such that the U.S. commercial space industry can field systems one generation ahead of international competitors and the U.S. Government can field systems two generations ahead. These goals can be attained if the U.S. Government is a responsible investor, consumer and regulator in the space industry. The U.S. Government needs to:

- Increase its space research and development *investment* and focus on those critical technologies unique to national security.

- Become a more reliable *customer* of commercial space products and services.

- Establish *regulatory* policies that encourage rather than restrict the availability of space products worldwide, while maintaining the U.S. technological lead.

Continued investment in research and development will help discover revolutionary and innovative advances for national security. At the same time, earlier-generation technology can migrate to the domestic and international commercial sectors.

3. New Approaches to Space

The cost of transporting payloads to space has two separate aspects: the cost-per-unit of weight and the cost-per-unit of capability. In the near term, it will be easier to reduce the cost-per-unit of capability, through miniaturization and related technologies, than to reduce the cost-per-unit of weight. Beyond these technical advances, mastery of space requires new approaches that will lower the cost of building and launching space systems.

Two fundamental changes could revolutionize U.S. space capabilities and lead the way to reducing the cost of operating in space:

- Align payload value to risk by separating manned space operations from cargo launches, making both manned and unmanned space operations more economical. For example, manned space flights could be supported by smaller reusable launch vehicles that incorporate the range of safety measures required for manned flights. On the other hand, cargo could be launched on more economical vehicles, either unmanned reusable launch vehicles or expendable vehicles, without the expensive, time-consuming safety measures required for manned flight.

- Shift from hand-tooled, custom-built space hardware to an infrastructure based on standardized hardware and software.

U.S. Objectives for Space

E. Create and Sustain a Cadre of Space Professionals

Since its inception, a hallmark of the U.S. space program has been world-class scientists, engineers and operators from academic institutions, industry, government agencies and the military Services. Sustained excellence in the scientific and engineering disciplines is essential to the future of the nation's national security space program. It cannot be taken for granted.

Military space professionals will have to master highly complex technology; develop new doctrine and concepts of operations for space launch, offensive and defensive space operations, power projection in, from and through space and other military uses of space; and operate some of the most complex systems ever built and deployed. To ensure the needed talent and experience, the Department of Defense, the Intelligence Community and the nation as a whole must place a high priority on intensifying investments in career development, education and training to develop and sustain a cadre of highly competent and motivated military and civilian space professionals.

1. Developing a Military Space Culture

The Department of Defense is not yet on course to develop the space cadre the nation needs.

The Department of Defense is not yet on course to develop the space cadre the nation needs. The Department must create a stronger military space culture, through focused career development, education and training, within which the space leaders for the future can be developed. This has an impact on each of the Services but is most critical within the Air Force.

Leadership

Leadership is a vital element in gaining mastery in any military area of endeavor. U.S. air power is the product of pilots such as Billy Mitchell, Hap Arnold and Curtis LeMay. It was Hyman Rickover who blazed the trail that led to the nuclear Navy. These individuals succeeded because they drew upon the talents of thousands of flyers or nuclear naval officers leading at all levels of command and staff. In the Air Force pilot and Navy nuclear submarine career fields, military leaders have spent about 90 percent of their careers within their respective fields.

In contrast, military leaders with little or no previous experience or expertise in space technology or operations often lead space organizations. A review by the Commission of over 150 personnel currently serving in key operational space leadership positions showed that fewer than 20 percent of the flag officers in key space jobs come from space career backgrounds (Figure 18). The remaining officers, drawn from pilot, air defense artillery and Intercontinental Ballistic Missile (ICBM) career fields, on average had spent 8 percent, or 2.5 years, of their careers in space or space related positions. Officers commanding space wings, groups and squadrons fare only slightly better; about one-third of the officers have extensive space experience, while the remaining two-thirds averaged less than 4.5 years in space-related positions (Figure 19).

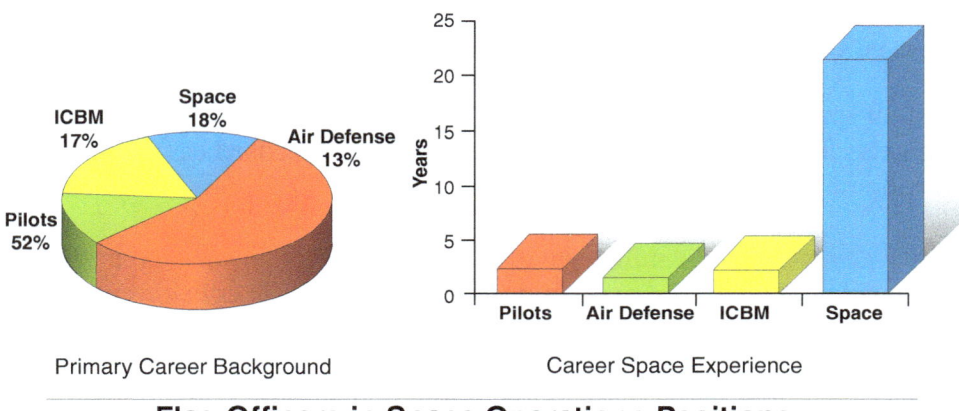

Flag Officers in Space Operations Positions
Source: Commission

Figure 18: Career space experience of flag officers

This lack of experience in leadership positions is a result of several factors. The space force is young and small, but it has been around long enough for a few to reach four-star rank and the number of personnel is growing. There has been an infusion of personnel from the ICBM force into space organizations in an effort to broaden career opportunities for the missile launch officers. Over time, this will create a larger cadre of space professionals, but in the short term it has had an impact on the overall level of experience of space personnel. Military officers with space training are in high demand in the commercial world. As a result, there has been a

U.S. Objectives for Space

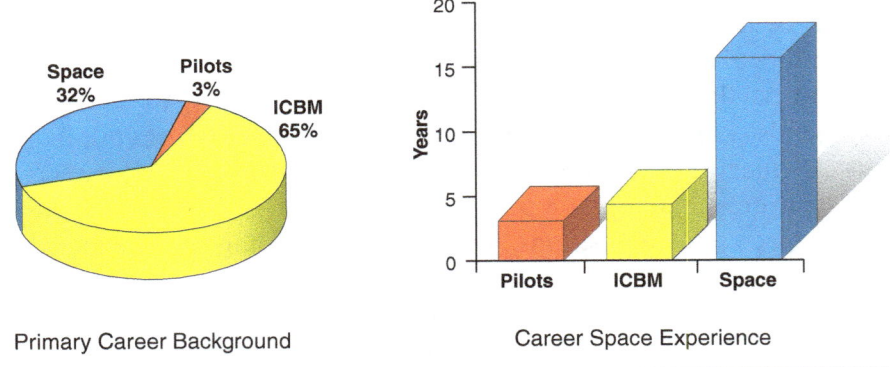

Field Grade Officers in Space Operations Positions
Source: Commission

Figure 19: Career space experience of Air Force field grade officers

drain of space talent as evidenced by the low retention of first term space engineers and operators. Finally, there is a lack of focused career development in the space community.

Space leadership in the military will require highly trained and experienced personnel at the very senior positions and throughout all echelons of command. These leaders must provide the vision, the technological expertise and doctrine, concepts and tactics to generate and operate space forces in this new era of space and to generate the cadre of space professionals future military operations will require. New space personnel management policies and new career paths are needed to develop leaders with greater depth and breath of experience in the space career field.

New Career Paths
Depth. Space professionals need more depth of experience in their field and more extensive education and training. In the past, space forces have relied on accessions of highly educated officers who are trained in space once in the job. Instead, career tracks need to be developed that will provide commanders at all levels more expertise within their mission areas. To achieve this, specific criteria should be developed for the selection, training, qualification and assignment of space personnel who will design, develop, acquire and operate military space systems. Training programs need to be refined to provide the basis for qualifying space professionals to occupy specific positions in the space force.

Breadth. Tomorrow's space professionals need a broader understanding of operations across the range of space mission areas and the size of the space cadre will need to grow, as space becomes increasingly important to military operations. Perhaps more than other areas, space benefits from a unique and close relationship among research, development, acquisition and operations, as spacecraft are usually procured in far fewer numbers, sometimes as few as one or two, than are tanks, airplanes or missiles. Exchange of personnel across space communities, between the operational and acquisition commands and between the Air Force and the NRO, is clearly desirable but at present there are barriers that restrict the cross flow of personnel among these communities.

Personnel managers in the Air Force need to have a comprehensive view of all space career positions within the national security space community and the means to manage individual assignments among the acquisition, operations and intelligence communities. Improving the exchange of personnel among these organizations, would expand the space manpower base and could also help to reverse the retention problem among space acquisition officers by opening up new career paths and leadership opportunities within the Air Force.

Education

To ensure the highly skilled workforce needed, technical education programs will have to be enhanced. Space systems under development, such as the Space-Based Infrared System and the Global Positioning System III, and future systems envisioned, such as a space-based radar and a space-based laser, will be far more complex than today's systems. New concepts for space launch, offensive and defensive space control operations and projection of military power in, from and through space will give rise to increasing technology innovation.

Other career fields, such as the Navy's nuclear submarine program, place strong emphasis on career-long technical education. This approach produces officers with a depth of understanding of the functions and underlying technologies of their systems that enables them to use the systems more efficiently in combat. The military's space force should follow this model. In addition, career field entry criteria should emphasize the need for technically oriented personnel, whether they be new lieutenants or personnel from related career fields. In-depth space-related science, engineering, application, theory and doctrine curricula should be developed and its study required for all military and government civilian space personnel, as is done in the Naval Nuclear Propulsion Program.

Tour Length

Military officers typically remain in their assignments for only a year or two, especially as they rise in rank. Short assignments can make it difficult for officers in leadership positions to establish sufficient continuity to create and execute a vision for the job. If the officers have experience and training in their specialties, however, problems of this sort can be mitigated.

In general, leadership in the space field today suffers on all counts: limited experience in the field, little technical education and tour lengths that average less than a year and a half. This keeps space organizations from reaching their potential. Space leaders spend most of their assignments learning about space rather than leading. This can weaken their effectiveness as military leaders, as they of necessity come to depend on civilian subordinates, whether civil servants or contractor personnel. Until space leaders have more extensive experience and technical training in space activities, longer and more stable tour lengths would be desirable.

2. Professional Military Education

Space capabilities are already integral to all traditional air, land and sea military operations. They have contributed to U.S. successes in conflicts during the past decade, from DESERT STORM in 1991 to the air campaign against Serbia in 1999. Soldiers, sailors, marines and airmen need an understanding of how space systems are integrated into nearly all military operations, particularly as new systems and applications emerge.

> *Professional military education does not stress the technical, operational or strategic application of space systems to combat operations.*

Programs in the four Services' professional military education institutions are key sources of space education programs. In all the military schools, space education is gaining in prominence. Within the Air Force, space education is now integrated into all phases of professional military education. New Air Force lieutenants who attend the Aerospace Basic Course are taught space fundamentals and how space systems are integrated into the tactical and operational levels of war. Other Service schools offer space electives as well as optional space focus areas. The Naval War College offers several elective courses allowing students at both its intermediate and senior service schools to focus on space. The Army Command and General Staff College offers a focused study program requiring 81 hours of space-related instruction. Students completing this program are awarded a special skill identifier qualifying them to serve in space-related positions in Army and Joint commands.

Despite the increased attention given to space within the military education system, the core curriculum does not stress, at the appropriate levels, the tactical, operational or strategic application of space systems to combat operations. Military commanders and their staffs continue to rely on "space support teams" assigned to them in time of crisis to advise on the use of space capabilities. Commanders would be better able to exploit the full range of combat capability at their disposal if they were educated from the beginning of their careers in the application of space systems.

3. Science and Engineering Workforce

To build a cadre of space professionals, the Department of Defense needs to draw on the nation's best scientists and engineers. However, both industry and the U.S. Government face substantial shortages in these fields and an aging workforce. Experienced personnel from the Apollo generation are nearing retirement and recruitment is difficult. The aerospace and defense industries overall have seen their appeal battered by declining stock prices, steady layoffs, program failures and cost and schedule overruns. Without a sufficient base of interesting, leading edge technology programs, it is increasingly difficult for both industry and government to attract and retain talent.

> *Senior leaders in the space industry are unanimous in identifying recruiting and retention of qualified people as their number one problem.*

Senior leaders in the space industry are unanimous in identifying recruiting and retention of qualified people as their number one problem. Their talent pool is aging and many experienced engineers are leaving industry. Filling the pipeline is a growing challenge, with the space industry being one of many sectors competing for the limited number of trained scientists and engineers.

The National Science Board recently reported that the U.S. has fewer science and engineering graduates than many major industrialized and emerging nations. At the same time, the demand for scientists and engineers is expected to increase in the next ten years at a rate almost four times that of all other occupations. The growing need for scientists and engineers is a national concern.

IV. Organizations that Affect National Security Space

The previous chapters identified U.S. national security interests in space and measures needed to advance them. This chapter describes the principal organizations involved in national security space activities, concentrating on the Executive Office of the President, the Department of Defense, the Intelligence Community and the Congress. It provides an assessment of how well this structure now serves the nation's interests in space.

A. Executive Office of the President

There is no single individual other than the President who can provide sustained and deliberate leadership, direction and oversight of national security space policy that is needed. Currently, responsibility and accountability for space are broadly diffused throughout the government.

The 1996 National Space Policy designates the National Science and Technology Council (NSTC), a Cabinet-level organization chaired by the President, as "the principal forum for resolving issues related to national space policy." The Office of Science and Technology Policy (OSTP) coordinates Federal policies for science and technology. The Director of OSTP also serves as the Assistant to the President for Science and Technology. In this role, he co-chairs the President's Committee of Advisors on Science and Technology and supports the NSTC. The policy directs that, "as appropriate, the NSTC and NSC [National Security Council] will co-chair policy processes."

In the National Security Council, national security space issues are currently assigned to the Senior Director for Defense Policy and Arms Control. Within this office, one staff member is assigned responsibility for space issues. This staff position supports the Senior Director for Intelligence on the NSC staff and also supports the Office of Science and Technology Policy on national security space issues.

This arrangement has not, does not and cannot provide the focused attention to space matters that is needed (Figure 20). The interdependence of the space sectors requires a more concentrated focus on space at the Cabinet level. The distribution of responsibility for space activity among many departments and agencies is less than ideal.

> *This arrangement has not, does not and cannot provide the focused attention to space matters that is needed.*

Organizations that Affect National Security Space

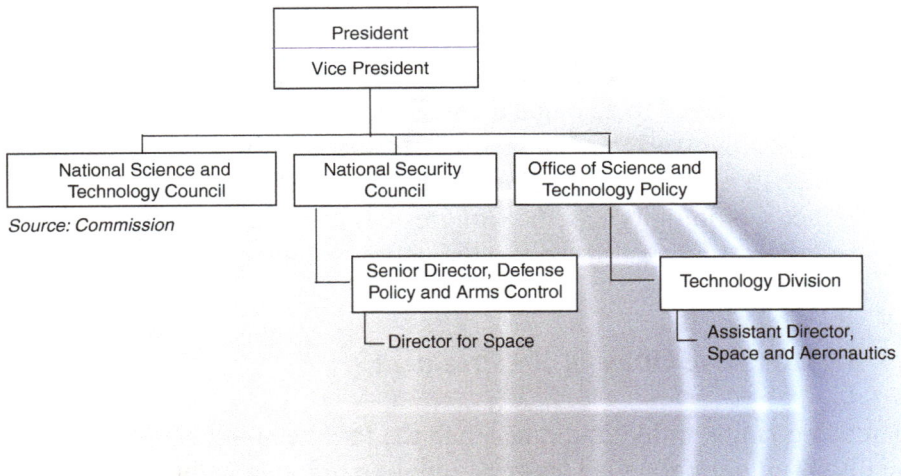

Figure 20: Current Organization for Space
Within the Executive Office of the President

Moreover, the portfolio of the Senior Director with responsibility for space affairs on the NSC is broad. That combined with a lack of staff support means that space issues are selectively addressed, frequently only when they have become crises.

For the last two years, the NSC staff has worked to resolve a number of critical issues, such as licensing for earth remote sensing satellite services, modernizing the GPS constellation and integrating the nation's civil and military weather satellite systems. This case-by-case approach, however, has not allowed the development of a coherent, persistent and deliberate national process for implementing U.S. national security space policy.

B. Department of Defense

1. Secretary of Defense

Title 10 of the U.S. Code, which provides the statutory basis for the Armed Services, assigns the Secretary of Defense as the principal assistant to the President in all matters relating to the Department of Defense. The Secretary has "authority, direction, and control" over the Department. With respect to those elements of the Intelligence Community within the Department, Title 50 U.S.C. provides the statutory basis for the Intelligence Community and directs that the Secretary, in consultation with the Director of Central Intelligence (DCI), "shall…ensure that [their] budgets are adequate…[and] ensure appropriate implementation of the policies and resource decisions of the Director of Central Intelligence by [those] elements…" This dual tasking establishes the obligation for the Secretary of Defense to ensure that the missions of the Department of Defense and of the Intelligence Community are successfully completed.

With respect to defense elements within the Intelligence Community, the DCI has the responsibility to "facilitate the development of an annual budget for intelligence and intelligence-related activities" and "establish the requirements and priorities to govern the collection of national intelligence by elements of the national intelligence community…" This includes those elements within the Department of Defense.

2. Office of the Secretary of Defense

The Deputy Secretary of Defense (DepSecDef) has generally been responsible for many aspects of the day-to-day management of the Department. On matters relating to space, the DepSecDef is usually involved in acquisition matters through the Under Secretary of Defense for Acquisition, Technology and Logistics, who serves as the Defense Acquisition Executive. As chairman of the Defense Resources Board, the DepSecDef is directly involved in budget decisions. With respect to intelligence, the DepSecDef and the DCI have historically conferred on policies, plans, programs and budgets for the Department of Defense and the Intelligence Community.

The relationship between the Secretary of Defense and the Director of Central Intelligence has evolved over time in such a manner that national security space issues do not receive the sustained focus appropriate to their importance to national security. Except for responding to urgent programmatic decisions, defense secretaries have generally delegated the management of national security space activities. Today, this responsibility is delegated to the Assistant Secretary of Defense for Command, Control, Communications, and Intelligence (ASD (C3I)), who serves as the "principal staff assistant and advisor to the Secretary and Deputy Secretary of Defense and the focal point within the Department for space and space-related activities" (Figure 21). The ASD (C3I) in turn relies on deputy assistant secretaries to guide policy and acquisition and provide oversight of the Department's intelligence, surveillance, reconnaissance, information, command, control, communications and space programs.

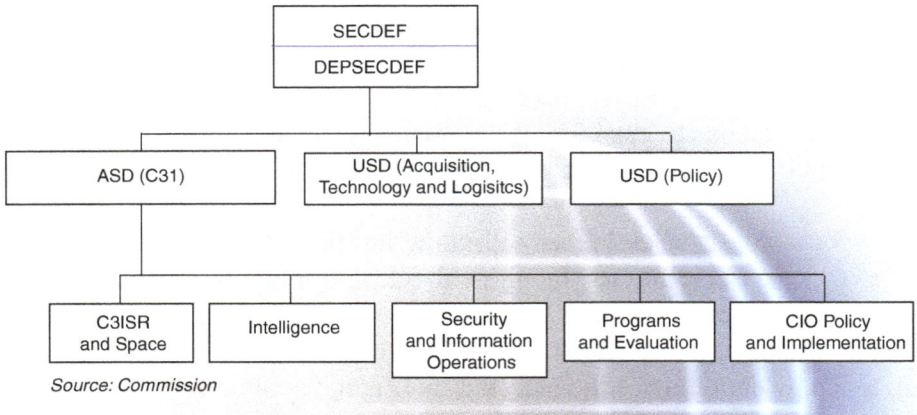

Figure 21: Current Organization for Space Within the Office of the Secretary of Defense

As established in the Department of Defense Space Policy, the ASD (C3I) coordinates space policy and acquisition with the appropriate Under Secretaries for Policy and for Acquisition, Technology and Logistics. In the role of principal staff assistant, the ASD (C3I) is charged with "authority, direction and control" of the Defense Intelligence Agency and Defense Security Service; "staff supervision" of the National Security Agency and the National Reconnaissance Office; and "overall supervision" of the National Imagery and Mapping Agency and the work of the National Security Space Architect (NSSA).

The ASD (C3I) also serves as the Chief Information Officer of the Department, and is the principal staff assistant in the Office of the Secretary of Defense (OSD) for developing, overseeing and integrating DoD policies and programs relating to the Department's information superiority strategy. In addition to space systems and space policy, ASD (C3I) functions include information policy and information management, command and control, communications, counterintelligence, security, information assurance, information operations, intelligence, surveillance and reconnaissance, and intelligence-related activities conducted by the Department.

The office of ASD (C3I) was first established in the early 1980s, restructured in the mid-1990s and restructured again in the late 1990s. Its development over time reflects an effort to provide a single point of responsibility for C3I within OSD. The evolving role for space in military operations, however, makes this difficult. Before the Gulf War, space capabilities were not well integrated into military operations. During and since the Gulf War, space has been seen as the place in which a combination of intelligence and surveillance sensors and command, control and communications systems could be based "to support the warfighter." The campaigns in Bosnia and Serbia extended the role for space. Information operations, which include the defense and attack of computer networks, were recognized as critical elements of military campaign planning. Many information operations are linked through satellites.

The scope of the ASD (C3I) portfolio reflects the difficult task of coordinating the many roles for space—national intelligence, support to the warfighter and information operations—across the many functions of DoD, which include policy, acquisition and interagency coordination. While concentrating responsibility in one office has advantages, the large number of issues to address and agencies to oversee and coordinate with results in a competition among them for the time and attention of the Assistant Secretary.

Within the organization, responsibility for space has devolved to a deputy assistant secretary. However, an official at this level does not have the rank to give space-related activities the visibility they need and to represent the Department in interagency fora.

In the office of the ASD (C3I), the Deputy Assistant Secretary of Defense for Programs and Evaluation is responsible for oversight of Service programming and budgeting for space-related C3I capabilities. It does not appear that this position has sufficient authority at the working level to influence policies that drive programming and budgeting decisions within the DoD.

The National Security Space Architect, who reports to both the ASD (C3I) and the head of the DCI's Community Management Staff, is charged with developing and coordinating space architectures that reflect the range of Intelligence Community and DoD space mission areas, with a view toward the mid- and long-term. However, the architect has no authority over the budgets or acquisition programs of the Services or the Intelligence Community.

The current ASD (C3I) organization suffers from three difficulties:

Organizations that Affect National Security Space

- The span of control is so broad that only the most pressing issues are attended to and space matters are left, on a day-to-day basis, in the hands of middle-level officials without sufficient influence within the Department and the interagency arena.

- Its influence on the planning, programming and budgeting process for space is too far removed or too late to have substantial effect on either the Services' or the Intelligence Community's processes.

- Within this structure, it is not possible for senior officials outside DoD to identify a single, high-level individual who has the authority to represent the Department on space-related matters.

3. Military Commanders in Chief (CINCs)

The nine CINCs are responsible for considering how space-based assets might be used to satisfy mission needs and how space capabilities and applications could be integrated into contingency and operational plans in their areas of responsibility. They also contribute to developing military requirements for space and space-related capabilities through the normal requirements process.

The CINCs are authorized to organize their forces as needed to carry out their assigned responsibilities. In recent military operations, the CINCs have organized functional commands for air, land and maritime operations. Future operations may well require a component commander for space due to the growing importance of space-based assets to combat operations.

4. Commander in Chief of U.S. Space Command and North American Aerospace Defense Command and Commander, Air Force Space Command

The Commander in Chief, U.S. Space Command (CINCSPACE) serves as the Commander in Chief, North American Aerospace Defense Command (CINCNORAD) and as the Commander, Air Force Space Command. As CINCSPACE, he serves as the advocate for the space requirements for all the CINCs and, on an annual basis, submits to the Chairman of the Joint Chiefs of Staff an Integrated Priority List that reflects these requirements. CINCSPACE has a broad set of responsibilities that are quite different in character. He is responsible for protecting and defending the space environment. His responsibilities also include support of strategic ballistic missile defense and DoD's computer network attack and computer network defense missions.

With the growing dependence on space and the vulnerability of space-related assets, more attention needs to be given to deploying and employing space-based capabilities for deterrence and defense. As space missions continue to expand, space will continue to mature as an "area of responsibility." All of this will require CINCSPACE to pay more attention to the space tasks assigned by the National Command Authorities, leaving less time for other assigned duties as CINCNORAD and Commander, Air Force Space Command.

5. Military Services

Each military Service is directed by the Secretary of Defense to execute specific space programs, comply with DoD space policy and integrate space capabilities into its strategy, doctrine, education, training, exercises and operations. Each Service is free to develop those space capabilities needed to perform its mission. However, no single Service has been assigned statutory responsibility to "organize, train and equip" for space operations. Eighty-five percent of space-related budget activity within the Department of Defense, approximately $7 billion per year, resides in the Air Force.

U.S. Air Force
The Air Force provides the facilities and bases, and operates and maintains its assigned space systems, to support the operational requirements of the U.S. Combatant Commands. These activities include surveillance, missile warning, nuclear detection, position, navigation, timing, weather and communications. The U.S. Air Force launches satellites for DoD and other government agencies and is responsible for air and missile defense and space control operations. The Air Force does not develop, acquire or operate the space-based reconnaissance satellites on which it and the other Services rely for precision, targeting, location and battlespace awareness. Those systems are developed, acquired and operated by the National Reconnaissance Office.

> *No single service has been assigned statutory responsibility to "organize, train and equip" for space operations.*

Organizations that Affect National Security Space

Within the Air Force, space-related activity is centered primarily in four elements (Figure 22). Space systems operations and requirements are organized under Air Force Space Command (AFSPC). The 14th Air Force launches the NRO, DoD and selected civil satellites and provides support for commercial satellite launches. The 14th Air Force also provides space-based support to the CINCs, and supports NORAD by providing missile warning and space surveillance information. Air Force Space Command develops all Air Force space requirements and works with the other Services in developing their requirements.

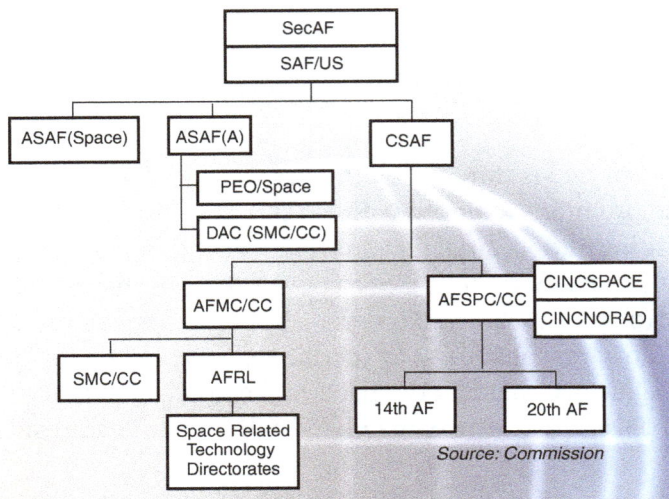

Figure 22: Current Organization for Space Within the Air Force

Design, development and acquisition of space launch, command and control, and satellite systems are conducted by personnel assigned to the Space and Missile Systems Center (SMC) under the Air Force Materiel Command. The Program Executive Officer (PEO) and the SMC Commander, who also serves as the Designated Acquisition Commander (DAC), report to the Assistant Secretary of the Air Force for Acquisition on the cost, schedule and performance for the programs in their portfolios. The Air Force Research Laboratory, also part of Air Force Materiel Command, conducts advanced technology research.

The Air Force role as the lead Service for space dates to the 1960s, with the creation of the Air Force Research and Development Command—the predecessor to Air Force Systems Command. The Air Force has since made a series of adjustments in the organization of its space activities. In many cases, these adjustments responded to a growth in responsibilities for space operations and space mission management. In 1982, for example, the Air Force Space Command was created because of growing dependence on space, the evolving threat from the Soviet Union, the growing space budget and a perceived need to "operationalize" space.

In the future, space will play an expanded role in transforming U.S. military forces; providing support to air, land and sea forces; conducting new missions of space surveillance; protecting space capabilities; and projecting power in, from, to and through space. These new missions will expand the Department's deterrence and defense capabilities into space.

Few witnesses before the Commission expressed confidence that the current Air Force organization is suited to the conduct of these missions. Nor was there confidence that the Air Force will fully address the requirement to provide space capabilities for the other Services. Many believe the Air Force treats space solely as a supporting capability that enhances the primary mission of the Air Force to conduct

> *As with air operations, the Air Force must take steps to create a culture within the Service dedicated to developing new space system concepts, doctrine and operational capabilities.*

offensive and defensive air operations. Despite official doctrine that calls for the integration of space and air capabilities, the Air Force does not treat the two equally. As with air operations, the Air Force must take steps to create a culture within the Service dedicated to developing new space system concepts, doctrine and operational capabilities.

U.S. Army

Space operations assigned to the Army are conducted by Army Space Command, an element of the Army's Space and Missile Defense Command (SMDC). Army Space Command is assigned as the Army component to U.S. Space Command. Army Space Command is assigned payload control responsibility for the Defense Satellite Communications System (DSCS) and operates Ground Mobile Forces terminals, providing DSCS communications to DoD forces forward deployed worldwide. The Army conducts space surveillance operations from Kwajalein Atoll in the Marshall Islands. Satellite terminal and receiver operations are spread throughout the Army, based in units responsible for a particular function. Joint Tactical Ground Stations are co-operated by the Army Space

Organizations that Affect National Security Space

Command and Naval Space Forces in Europe, Korea and the Middle East. Army intelligence units assigned worldwide operate a variety of terminals and receivers that collect and receive space, air and ground intelligence.

The Department of the Army Headquarters approves Army space requirements developed by SMDC's Force Development Integration Center. However, Army Space Command and the Army Training and Doctrine Command also influence the development of Army space requirements. Research, development and acquisition of space-related equipment are generally conducted within the Space and Missile Defense Command, the Intelligence and Security Command or the Communications Electronic Command. The Army Space Program Office has responsibility for the operation of systems acquired through the Army's Tactical Exploitation of National Capabilities (TENCAP) program.

U.S. Navy
Naval Space Command serves as the naval component of U.S. Space Command. Its responsibilities include operating assigned space systems for surveillance and warning; providing spacecraft telemetry and on orbit engineering; developing space plans, programs, concepts and doctrine; and advocating naval warfighting requirements in the joint arena. Space research and development in the Navy is conducted by the Naval Research Laboratory. Space requirements for the Navy and Marine Corps are developed by Naval Space Command; space systems are acquired by the Space and Naval Warfare Systems Command. The Navy also maintains a small TENCAP office to enhance warfighter use of national security space information.

Naval Space Command serves as the Alternate Space Command Center to U.S. Space Command's primary center located at Cheyenne Mountain, Colorado. It is also responsible for operating the Navy Radar Fence, which contributes to space surveillance. The Navy operates the UHF Follow-On constellation of communication satellites, is responsible for the development and acquisition of its replacement system, the Multi User Objective System, and acquires Navy ground terminals. The primary mission of Naval Space Command is to provide direct space support to Fleet and Fleet Marine Force operational units around the world, whether for routine deployments, exercises or crisis response.

6. National Reconnaissance Office

The National Reconnaissance Office (NRO) is the single national organization tasked to meet the U.S. Government's intelligence needs for space-borne reconnaissance. The NRO is responsible for unique and innovative technology; large-scale systems engineering; development, acquisition and operation of space reconnaissance systems; and related intelligence activities needed to support national security missions. While the NRO is an agency of the Department of Defense, its budget, the National Reconnaissance Program (NRP), is one part of the National Foreign Intelligence Program (NFIP). The Director of Central Intelligence provides guidance for and approves the NRP and all other elements of the NFIP. The Secretary of Defense ensures implementation of the DCI resource decisions by DoD elements within the NFIP. As a result, the NRO is a joint venture between these organizations.

> *The NRO today is a different organization, simultaneously struggling to manage a large number of legacy programs while working to renew a focus on leading edge research.*

The NRO had a reputation as one of the U.S. Government's best system acquisition agencies and worked to maintain exceptional systems engineering capabilities. In its early years, the NRO was a small, agile organization, a leader in developing advanced technologies, often first-of-a-kind systems, for solving some of the nation's most difficult intelligence collection challenges. The NRO today is a different organization, simultaneously struggling to manage a large number of legacy programs while working to renew a focus on leading edge research. The NRO's capacity to convert leading edge research and technology into innovative operational systems is inhibited by the requirement to maintain its legacy programs.

The NRO has been very successful in collecting intelligence globally and, as a result, customers have become increasingly dependent on the products from satellite reconnaissance. The NRO has spent an increasing amount of time operating and maintaining a large number of legacy satellite reconnaissance programs. To minimize the risk of disruption in service to its customers in this resource-constrained environment, the NRO's plans for new system acquisitions tend to stress operational utility and reliability, while reducing technical risk. This approach has the effect of favoring evolutionary improvements to current systems and less focus on developing new systems that incorporate revolutionary technical advances.

C. Intelligence Community

The Director of Central Intelligence is the principal advisor to the President for intelligence matters related to national security and serves as the head of the Intelligence Community. The DCI is responsible for providing national intelligence to the President, to the heads of departments and agencies of the executive branch, to the Chairman of the Joint Chiefs of Staff and senior military commanders and, when appropriate, to the Congress. "National intelligence" refers to "intelligence which pertains to the interests of more than one department or agency of the government."

The elements of the Intelligence Community include: the Office of the Director of Central Intelligence; the Central Intelligence Agency; the National Security Agency; the Defense Intelligence Agency; the National Imagery and Mapping Agency; the National Reconnaissance Office; other offices within DoD for the collection of specialized national intelligence through reconnaissance programs; the intelligence elements of the Army, Navy, Air Force, Marine Corps, Federal Bureau of Investigation, Department of the Treasury and Department of Energy; and the Department of State's Bureau of Intelligence and Research (Figure 23).

The DCI develops and presents to the President an annual budget for the National Foreign Intelligence Program, which is distributed throughout the budgets of the various departments and agencies that comprise the Intelligence Community.

The Community Management Staff, managed by the Deputy Director of Central Intelligence for Community Management, assists the DCI in coordinating and managing the Intelligence Community, including responsibility for managing resources and collection requirements and assessing space programs and policies. It is also responsible for coordinating policy and budgets with the Office of the Secretary of Defense. The Community Management Staff has made substantial progress in coordinating the planning and budgeting of the components of the Intelligence Community. However, it does not have authority to reprogram in-year money within components, an authority that would enhance its direction of Intelligence Community affairs. Nor is it well structured to coordinate with OSD on broad intelligence policy, long-term space strategy and other issues requiring intelligence support.

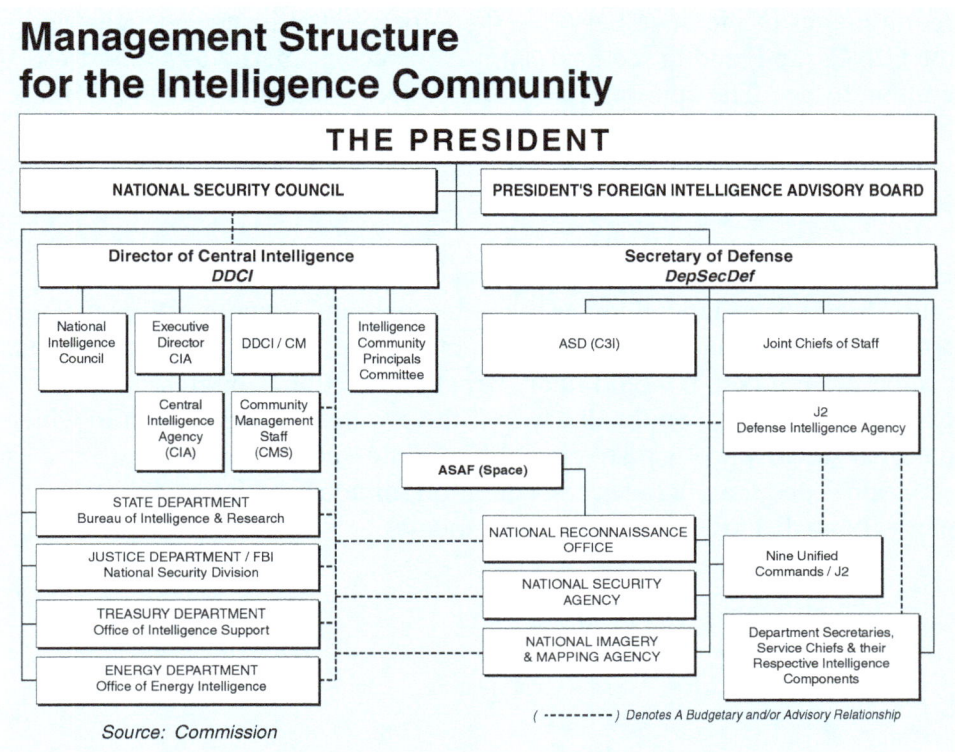

Figure 23: Current Intelligence Community Management Structure

D. Congress

Congressional oversight of the authorization and appropriation of national security space funding routinely involves no fewer than six committees. These include the House and Senate Armed Services Committees (HASC/SASC), the House and Senate Appropriations Committees (HAC/SAC), the Senate Select Committee on Intelligence (SSCI) and the House Permanent Select Committee on Intelligence (HPSCI), as well as the Budget Committees. Four or five committees review DoD space programs; six committees review intelligence space programs. For example, the HPSCI reviews the Joint Military Intelligence Program and the Tactical Intelligence and Related Activities program; the SSCI does not. While an exception, some civil space activities can be reviewed by as many as 13 committees.

Organizations that Affect National Security Space

Generally, each committee mirrors the priorities of the executive branch interests it oversees. The intelligence committees focus on issues concerning "sources and methods" and on the ability of the Intelligence Community to provide intelligence to the National Command Authorities. The Armed Services committees contend with competing space requirements of the three Services, the military intelligence agencies and the CINCs, and tend to see national intelligence primarily as support for combat forces. The appropriations committees' subcommittees on defense oversee all defense and intelligence space programs and are one place where national security space programs are viewed together. However, they focus primarily on budgets.

Executive branch officials must expend considerable time and energy interacting with a large number of committees and subcommittees that, on some matters, have overlapping jurisdiction. To the extent that this process can be streamlined, it would likely benefit the nation, Congress and the executive branch. It would also help if there were an environment in which national security space matters could be addressed as an integrated program—one that includes consideration for commercial and civil capabilities that are often overlooked today.

V. Management of National Security Space Activities

A number of issues transcend organizational approaches and are important to the ability of the U.S. to achieve its objectives in space. These are issues that the national leadership, the Department of Defense and the Intelligence Community should address in the near term, irrespective of particular organizational arrangements that may be pursued. Resolution of them would both benefit and support organizational changes.

A. Interagency Coordination

1. Current Interagency Process

The current interagency process is inadequate for the volume and complexity of today's space issues. For the most part, the existing interagency process addresses space issues on an as needed basis. As issues in the space arena inevitably become more complex, this approach will become increasingly unsatisfactory. What may be needed is a standing interagency group to identify key national security space issues, to guide, as necessary, the revision of existing national space policy and to oversee implementation of that policy throughout the departments and agencies of the U.S. Government. The need for a standing interagency coordination process is made more urgent by the fact that there are a number of pending issues on space affairs in Congress, in domestic regulatory bodies and in international trade and arms control negotiating fora. To avoid unintended and deleterious effects on the space sectors, these issues must be addressed in a comprehensive fashion.

2. Pending Agenda

The domestic and international issues facing the U.S. demand a coherent policy approach and deliberate direction for their treatment. A sample of that agenda includes:

- Arms control issues that China, Russia, Greece and Pakistan have raised in the United Nations Committee on Peaceful Uses of Outer Space.

- World Trade Organization negotiations regarding market access for commercial satellite systems.

- Domestic allocation of spectrum for third generation wireless (scheduled to occur by July 1, 2001) and the potential authorization of commercial ultrawide band services (a pending Federal Communications Commission rulemaking proceeding), both of which may affect DoD use of spectrum for military operations, government use of commercial spectrum and commercial use of government spectrum.

- Claims of developing countries regarding equitable access to radio frequency spectrum and orbital locations.

- U.S. and international development of orbital debris and deorbiting policies.

- Domestic licensing issues involving commercial, civil and national security interests, such as remote sensing policies, export control and foreign ownership.

B. SecDef/DCI Relationship

No relationship within the executive branch touching on national security space is as important as the one between the Secretary of Defense and the Director of Central Intelligence.

> *No relationship...touching on national security space is as important as the one between the Secretary of Defense and the Director of Central Intelligence.*

Together, the Secretary and the DCI control national security space capabilities. Neither can accomplish the tasks assigned without the support of the other. The Secretary's support is needed by the DCI to field and operate intelligence systems. The DCI provides much of the intelligence required by the Secretary to support the development of U.S. military capabilities and the conduct of military operations. The Secretary's interest in and support of intelligence is critical to the DCI. The higher the Secretary's level of interest, the closer the relationship with the DCI is likely to be as the two work to assure the development and fielding of systems and the conduct of operations essential to the nation's security.

Since the two positions were created in 1947, and especially since the NRO was created in 1960, the relationship between the two officials has varied. While the Secretary and the DCI have established processes through which to cooperate on routine national security issues, they have not given the national security space program their sustained, joint attention for nearly a decade. Nor have the urgent issues related to space control, information operations and the assessment of the threats the nation faces from space received the attention they deserve. Specifically, the U.S. must:

- Invest in advanced technologies.

- Exploit the commercial market to supply imagery to relieve the burden on national systems.

- Make revolutionary changes in the nation's intelligence collection systems.

- Develop space-based systems to meet pressing military requirements.

The Secretary and the DCI need to align their respective staff offices so that coordination on intelligence issues broadly, and space matters specifically, is easier and more direct between the two. There is no systemic organizational impediment to such alignment or to meeting the need for increased attention to critical issues. It is a matter of the priorities of the Secretary and the DCI and how they choose to delegate and oversee responsibilities for space-related concerns.

C. Acquiring and Operating Space Systems

The Department of Defense and the Intelligence Community acquire and operate most of the satellites used to support defense and intelligence missions. Within DoD, the Air Force is the Service that acquires most of the Department's satellites; the National Reconnaissance Office is the acquisition agent for the Intelligence Community's satellites. The two organizations have approached satellite acquisition and operations differently over time, although the processes have evolved in a similar fashion in recent years. Understanding the differences, however, is useful in evaluating alternatives to organizing and managing these functions in the future.

1. Budgeting

The DoD and NRO processes for assembling and approving budgets are similar. In DoD the Services identify the resources, including the funds, people and facilities, needed to support approved system requirements. The Services' space inputs are generated by their respective Space Commands, reviewed by Service Headquarters staffs, submitted by Service Secretaries, integrated and rationalized by the OSD staff through a structured process, and approved by the Secretary of Defense. In the NRO, the inputs are generated by its directorates; reviewed, integrated and rationalized by its staff; and submitted by the Director of the National Reconnaissance Office (DNRO) for DCI approval.

2. Satellite Acquisition

For acquisition, the DoD approval chain is from the program managers, to the Program Executive Officers, to the Component Acquisition Executive. In the NRO, the approval chain is from the program managers, to the directorate heads, to the Service Assistant Secretary for Acquisition and the DNRO. For major DoD programs, such as satellite systems, the Defense Acquisition Executive is the final decision authority. For all NRO programs, the DNRO is delegated the final decision authority, eliminating one layer of bureaucracy and the accompanying staff review.

Both the Air Force and the NRO acquire space systems under authorities from the Secretary of Defense (Figure 24). For some purposes unique to its mission, the NRO also operates under authorities derived from the Director of the Central Intelligence Agency, as provided for in the Central Intelligence Agency Act of 1949, as amended. The DoD acquisition process is described in Department of Defense Directive 5000.1 and applies to all major systems. In the early 1990s, the Deputy Secretary of Defense exempted the NRO from DoD Directive 5000.1 and directed the development of an equivalent process, known as Directive 7. Directive 7, in essence, tailored the basic principles in 5000.1 specifically for the acquisition of space systems, the NRO's only line of business, which resulted in a more streamlined process than that of the DoD. In the fall of 2000, however, DoD revised its 5000.1 directive to streamline the DoD acquisition process. It is now similar to the Directive 7 process.

Management of National Security Space Activities

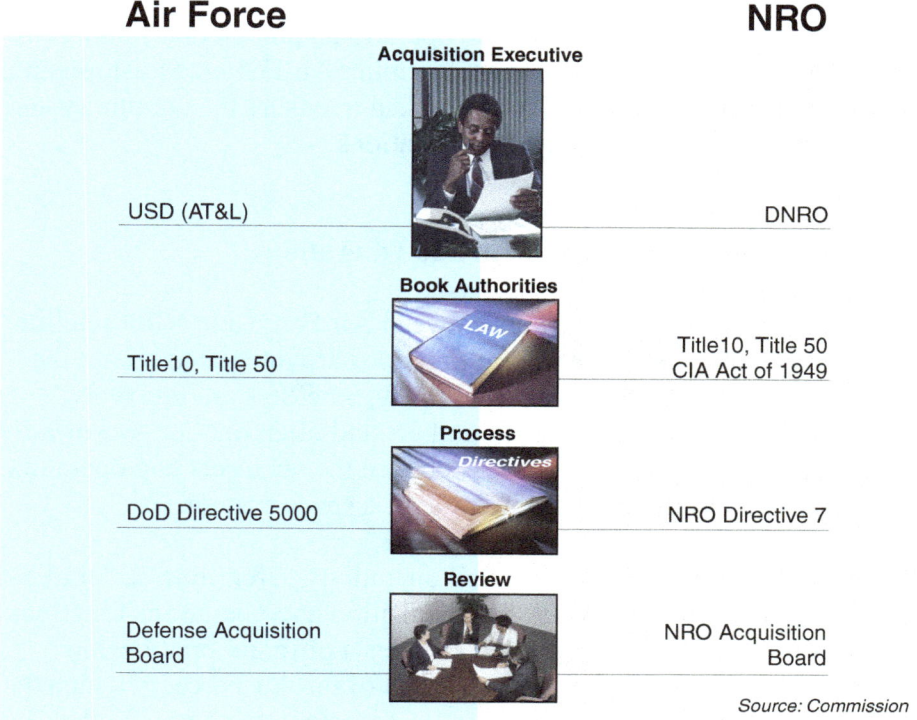

Figure: 24 Acquisition Oversight in the Air Force and the NRO

3. Satellite Operations

The use of NRO and Air Force satellites is sufficiently different that the approach to operations in the two organizations is also different in character. With the exception of station keeping and repositioning, operations of DoD satellites are characterized for the most part by constancy of operations. Operators monitor but do not interact with the satellites unless there is an anomaly. In contrast, NRO satellite operations are tasked frequently in response to constantly changing collection requirements. Operators intervene in real-time on a routine basis, often with each orbit of the satellite, to change the satellite configuration. These characteristics demand continuity of highly experienced, on-site technical experts who are extremely knowledgeable about the satellite design features. To support these requirements, NRO satellite operations rely on crews comprised of a government lead and a crew of contractor technical experts. However, DoD satellite operations rely less on contractor technical support at the ground stations.

Management of National Security Space Activities

Future DoD systems like the Space Based Infrared System will operate more like NRO systems. Therefore, the operational philosophies of the two organizations are likely to become more similar. Air Force acquisition and operations will have to be more closely linked to ensure the continuity and technical expertise needed in the ground stations.

4. Integrated Acquisition and Operations

While there are growing similarities between Air Force and NRO satellite acquisition and operations, how these functions are integrated within the two organizations is still quite different today. Satellites are relatively unique systems, purchased in small numbers and often one- or two-of-a-kind. As a result, a close relationship between the acquirers and operators can be beneficial throughout the life cycle of a space system.

The NRO's approach to acquisition and operations, referred to as "cradle-to-grave," more closely integrates the acquisition and operations functions within the organization. This approach creates a different relationship between the acquirers and operators than that of the Air Force, in which the acquisition and operations elements are in separate commands. In the NRO model, the individuals involved in acquiring the satellites are the same individuals who fly the satellites. Therefore, the experiences and understanding derived from operations can more directly influence satellite design; the reverse is also true. When the operators are on the technical design team, their capacity to resolve on-orbit anomalies during satellite operation is greater. This is not the case in the Air Force, where the operators have less direct influence in design. These differences amount, in essence, to different organizational cultures within NRO and Air Force space activities, an understanding of which is essential to determining whether and how the activities might be integrated over time.

D. Pursuing "Leap Ahead" Technologies

Technology has been a major driver of U.S. economic growth over the past five decades. Scientific discovery and technological innovation have been important elements of U.S. economic and military leadership, and have improved the quality of life in the United States. Technological superiority has aided the U.S. military in maintaining its worldwide commitments even as the size of its force has been reduced. As the spread of high technology weaponry on the world market continues, it will become increasingly difficult to stay ahead, particularly in space-related technologies. The Department of Defense needs to provide both resources and direction to ensure that advances in space technology continue.

1. Managing Science and Technology Programs

Declining budgets and programmatic instability have had a major impact on key technologies required by the defense and intelligence space sectors. For example, the U.S. has lost its preeminence in rocket propulsion technology. A review by the Defense Science and Technology Advisory Group in 1999 concluded that funding perturbations could potentially decimate one of the nation's priority propulsion initiatives. For example, the U.S. will rely on Russian RD-180 technology to power some of its core Evolved Extended Launch Vehicle (EELV) booster fleet. In addition to losing preeminence in space booster technology, the Air Force Scientific Advisory board declared in 1995 that "other countries have taken the lead in spacecraft propulsion, where U.S. technology is behind what has been accomplished in the former Soviet Union."

Certain core technologies rely on a narrow industrial base. The U.S. Government may need to sustain critical providers through innovative programs such as "centers of excellence." Radiation-hardened parts and atomic clocks are two examples of the larger problem of an eroding industrial base. In each of these cases, the business base is inadequate to sustain the companies that supply the components. In the case of radiation-hardened parts, market forecasts project a decline in the business base of 50 to 60 percent. The sole U.S. company that produces the atomic clock critical to the U.S. GPS system announced in 2000 that it plans to stop production because of insufficient market demand.

The Department needs to actively coordinate science and technology investments across the space technology community so as to better integrate and prioritize these efforts, many of which have application across all space sectors. The defense and intelligence sectors need to partner more closely with the civil sector. Some NASA research and development programs have national security applications. Investments in launch infrastructure and launch vehicles have clear applications across all sectors.

Many attempts have been made, but with limited success, to coordinate space technology planning, development and projects among the various space technology communities. In 1997, the Space Technology Alliance, an informal organization with membership that includes executive-level technical directors from NASA, DoD, the Intelligence Community and others, was established to coordinate the development of space technologies. This has done much to improve the level of interagency coordination, but even so, a number of priority national issues need attention at a higher level. Modernization of U.S. launch ranges and the development of a reusable launch vehicle, both of which are key drivers to reducing the cost of access to space for government and commercial purposes, are critical examples.

2. Space Technology Goals

The Department of Defense should focus its space technology investment strategy on:

- Reducing the cost of launch and space systems by emphasizing miniaturization and new ways of doing business (Figures 25).

- Developing new sensors that can detect and track smaller, moving and concealed targets under all environmental conditions.

- Promoting on-orbit data processing and artificial intelligence to reduce human operator costs and the burden of high data volume on the communications infrastructure.

- Developing advanced launcher and propulsion technology to reduce the cost of getting to and maneuvering on orbit.

- Developing on-orbit servicing equipment that can extend space system life expectancy and makes it possible to upgrade system capabilities on orbit.

- Developing advanced surveillance and defensive and offensive technologies needed for space control and information operations (Figures 26).

- Developing advanced command and control, guidance and pointing, power generation, materials and optics technologies needed for power projection from space.

Management of National Security Space Activities

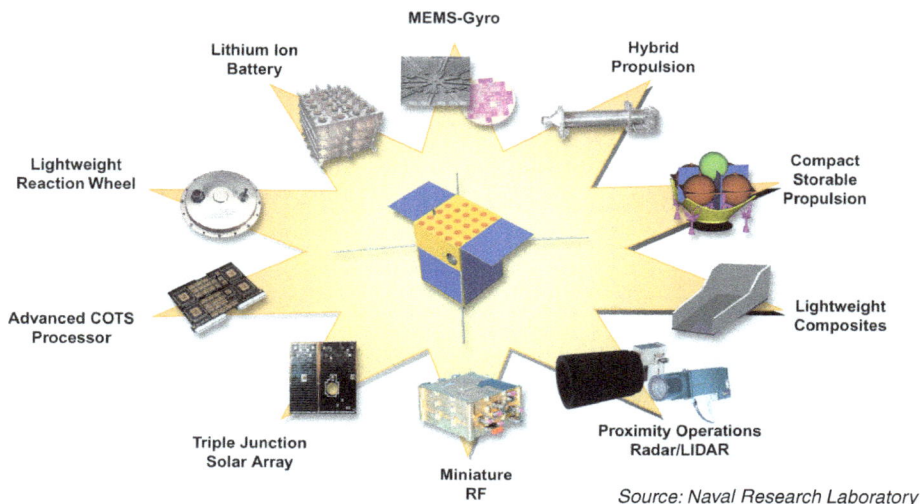

Figure 25: Examples of advanced space system technologies

In addition to establishing possible areas for investment, the Department, in cooperation with the space community, needs to ensure that an environment exists within which experimentation and innovation will flourish. Most successful science and technology programs are conducted in organizations well apart from the bureaucratic mainstream. It would serve the space community well to establish temporary joint interagency program offices to foster flexible, innovative and adaptable space technology research and development.

Source: Air Force Space Command
Figure 26: Artist rendering of the space based laser demonstration project, now in research and development.

E. Leveraging the Commercial and Civil Sectors

The commercial and civil space sectors provide satellite services and scientific and engineering resources useful for national security space. In the United States, investments from commercial space activities now exceed those of the U.S. Government by a factor of two. For decades, in conflict and in peacetime, the Department of Defense and the Intelligence Community have turned to the commercial industry to develop new technologies, design new systems and build hardware. They rely as well on industry to provide services, such as satellite communication and imagery services, when U.S. Government capabilities cannot meet requirements (Figure 27).

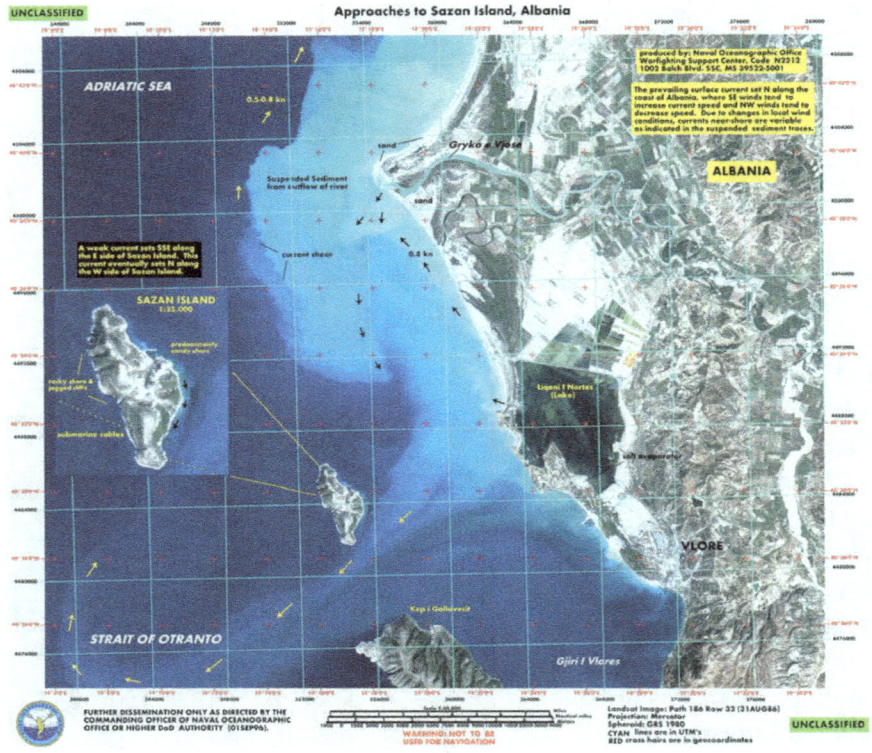

Source: Naval Oceanographic Office Warfighter Support Center, Stennis Space Center, Mississippi (Approved for Public Release)
Figure 27: U.S. military forces use commercial imagery for "intelligence preparation of the battlefield"

Despite the importance of the U.S. commercial and civil space sectors to the successful completion of the national security mission, the U.S. Government has no comprehensive approach to incorporating those capabilities and services into its national security space architecture. Nor does it have well-defined policies to enhance the competitiveness of the commercial and civil industries. The U.S. Government, as a consumer, a regulator or an investor, is currently not a good partner to the national security space industry.

> *The U.S. Government, as a consumer, a regulator or an investor, is currently not a good partner to the national security space industry.*

1. Launch Facilities

Air Force launch facilities continue to support both government and commercial launches, even as the number of commercial launches from these facilities approaches half of the total. Privatizing the maintenance and operations of the launch infrastructure is a valid consideration as long as the U.S. Government retains control of certain core governmental functions, such as making critical safety decisions on destroying a rocket that has strayed off course. The commercial sector is gaining experience in space operations. Three states, New Mexico, Virginia and Alaska, are developing spaceports to handle commercial and government customers. In October 1996, NASA began the transfer of responsibility for day-to-day operations and management of the U.S. Space Shuttle fleet to United Space Alliance, a commercial space operations company, while retaining oversight of the Space Shuttle program. The Department of Transportation is responsible for issuing licenses to private companies to provide commercial space payload processing and launch services at the two government launch sites.

2. Export Control Policy

Except where exclusions are needed for national security purposes, U.S. Government policies should encourage the U.S. commercial space sector to earn as much of the international commercial space market as possible. U.S. industry, therefore, deserves timely responses from the U.S. Government in approval or denial of licenses. Unfortunately, the current process produces long delays in licensing approval. The Canadian government, for example, originally intended to award a contract to build Radarsat 2 to a U.S. company, but awarded it instead to an Italian company because of U.S. export control procedures and regulations. Industry reports many instances in which it took months to get permission to hold a meeting with a close U.S. ally, and in one case took weeks to get permission to make a phone call to a foreign entity. This sort of delay is damaging to U.S. industry in today's fast-paced, international markets. The U.S Government must develop and evolve new export control and licensing processes that will promote the commercial space industry, while being mindful of national security considerations.

3. Satellite Services

The U.S. Government and its allies have turned to the commercial sector for many satellite services and products and will continue to do so (Figure 28). Among the many examples of commercial products used by the U.S. Government are these:

- In 1991, the U.S. military procured commercial remote sensing imagery from a non-U.S. company during Desert Storm. Commercial satellite communications services were critical to U.S. Army missions.

- In 1995, the U.S. Navy bought more than two million minutes of service on an intergovernmental satellite system constellation, and many Navy ships communicate through the system today.

- The U.S. Government has leveraged commercially-developed direct broadcast satellite technology for its Global Broadcast Service.

Source: Air Force Space Warfare Center
Figure 28: The U.S. military uses commercial satellite communications to support its missions.

The Department of Defense and the Intelligence Community are not likely to own and operate enough on-orbit assets to meet their requirements. According to RAND Corporation, "in the near term, there are not enough military systems to satisfy projected communications demand and commercial systems will have to be used." The Department of Defense uses commercial services on a daily basis. However, it often procures these services on an ad hoc basis rather than integrating them into its space architecture planning process because of a concern over potential unavailability in a crisis situation. Furthermore, the Department builds capabilities that could perhaps be more economically provided by the commercial sector.

Besides satisfying DoD needs, greater use of commercial satellite systems also could facilitate more effective operations with U.S. allies by providing greater interoperability between some U.S. and non-U.S. military satellite systems. The U.S. Government should become a more reliable customer for commercial products and should plan to augment internal capabilities with commercial products and services in developing future space architectures. The Department of Defense should buy commercial services and products unless a unique requirement can be justified.

4. Multinational Space Alliances

Multinational alliances can increase U.S. space capabilities and reduce costs, as well as give the U.S. access to foreign investment, technology and expertise. Fostering these alliances can help maintain the U.S. position as a leader in the global space market. Civil multinational alliances provide opportunities for the United States to promote international cooperation and build support among other countries, especially emerging space-faring nations and developing countries, for U.S. positions on international policy or regulatory concerns.

F. Budgeting for Space

Currently, there is no DoD appropriation that identifies and aggregates funding for space programs. Space funding is a part of many appropriations spread across DoD and Intelligence Community budgets. Most of the funding for national security space is in the Air Force and National Reconnaissance Office budgets. The Army and Navy each fund space programs that are primarily in support of Service-unique requirements. The Army funds common user and Army-unique ground terminals, and the Navy funds the UHF Follow-On program, the Multi-User Objective System and Navy terminals. These multiple appropriations lead to several problems:

- When satellite programs are funded in one budget and terminals in another, the decentralized arrangement can result in program disconnects and duplication. It can result in lack of synchronization in the acquisition of satellites and their associated terminals.

- It can also be difficult for user requirements to be incorporated into the satellite system if the organization funding the system does not agree with and support those user requirements.

- Since the Air Force builds most DoD space systems, the Army and the Navy fund little research and development for space.

Of some concern is that, although the Army and the Navy represent DoD's largest users of space products and capabilities, their budget activities consistently fail to reflect the importance of space. Their rationale is that space technology programs should be funded by the Air Force. This dichotomy between the importance of space to the Army and the Navy versus the funding commitment these Services make needs to be addressed.

The current method of budgeting for national security space programs lacks the visibility and accountability essential to developing a coherent program. Alternative budget mechanisms, such as a major force program or space appropriation, would be useful in raising the visibility of the national security space program in the Department of Defense's budgeting process.

1. Major Force Program

A Major Force Program (MFP) is a tool to track program resources independent of Congressional appropriations. Currently, 11 such MFPs cover functional areas such as strategic programs, general-purpose forces, guard and reserve, and airlift. Each MFP is further broken into program elements that track dollars and people across the various appropriations assigned to a particular program, such as the F-22 aircraft, the DDG-51 destroyer and the UH-60 helicopter. While there are program elements dedicated to particular space programs, such as SBIRS or the EELV, there is no MFP for space and related programs, nor is there any comprehensive effort in DoD to identify all space and related ground elements.

All MFPs, except MFP 11, are managed decentrally. In the case of MFP 11 for special operations forces, the Congress directed that management control of those resources be exercised by the Commander in Chief, U.S. Special Operations Command.

2. Space Appropriation

An alternative approach is to consolidate space programs in specific Congressional appropriations. For example, there are such appropriations for Air Force aircraft, for Army military personnel and for Navy shipbuilding. No similar appropriation exists for space programs, even in the Air Force. While an appropriation effectively "fences" programs by Service or defense agency, it does not necessarily provide insight into the dynamics of the individual programs.

G. Exercises, Experiments and Wargames

The military uses a variety of tools to simulate warfighting environments in support of exercises, experiments and wargames. However, these tools have not been modernized to take into account the missions and tasks that space systems can perform. As a result, simulation tools cannot be used as effectively to understand the utility of space-based capabilities on warfare.

1. Exercises

Military exercises generally involve training with current capabilities. To the extent feasible, Service and joint exercises train forces for missions they may be called upon to perform during conflict. Incorporating actual space capabilities into exercises is difficult. Intelligence satellites can provide some products in real time, but because training objectives are usually scripted, synthetic intelligence products are often used. Because doing so would shorten their operational lives, satellites are rarely moved to accommodate the requirements of an exercise. Because of potential loss of control of the satellite, ground stations are not disabled. Nor are satellites such as GPS jammed, because to do so would interrupt their real world missions.

Space capabilities should be embedded in military exercises.

As a result, military commanders have had relatively little experience in learning to cope with the loss or temporary interruption of key space capabilities, such as GPS, satellite communications, remote sensing or missile warning information. Space capabilities should be embedded in military exercises. The 527th Space Aggressor Squadron, created in October 2000 by the Air Force, is the kind of capability that could be incorporated into exercises to demonstrate the impact of warfighting operations on hostile actions directed against space-based capabilities.

2. Experiments

Experiments are conducted primarily to evaluate prototypes or upgraded capabilities. Service battle labs and research organizations have conducted experiments involving space applications for years. These experiments have made possible new capabilities such as near real-time imagery transmitted to the cockpit, space-based tracking of friendly forces and dissemination of missile warning data. Most space experiments tend to be conducted by a single Service, despite the fact that space systems support joint missions. Experiments need to focus more on joint applications. A Space Applications Experimentation Cell at Joint Forces Command could provide the leadership needed to encourage more innovative experiments for this purpose.

3. Wargames

Wargames, unlike exercises and experiments, are devised to examine future concepts. These are particularly applicable to concepts relating to space, in which satellite constellations costing tens of billions of dollars can be simulated with a few keystrokes. The Services, OSD and NRO conduct wargames that address vital emerging national security space concepts and issues. These activities should be expanded to include greater participation of senior-level officials from the national security community. Standardizing the force structures and timeframes examined within the different wargames would be useful to enable comparisons of the lessons learned in various games. More should be done to ensure that NRO wargaming capabilities are included in Service, joint and combined wargames to foster greater collaboration on future space system concepts.

4. Models and Simulation

The Department of Defense uses models and simulation to help develop system requirements, test new system concepts, plan acquisition and conduct useful but less expensive training. Historically, DoD has measured the potential combat effectiveness of new systems by simulating their employment in mock combat. Because the value of communications, intelligence and space systems can be difficult to quantify, their contributions to warfighting are not accurately captured in current models and simulations. To support exercises, experiments and wargames, the Department must develop and employ modeling and simulation tools based on measures of merit and effectiveness that will quantify the effects of space-based capabilities.

VI. Organizing and Managing for the Future

National security space organization and management today fail to reflect the growing importance of space to U.S. interests. The Defense Science Board Task Force on Space Superiority observed that "the use of space has become such a dominant factor in the outcome of future military conflict and in the protection of vital national security interests that it should take on the priority...similar to that which existed for Strategic Forces in the 1960s through 1980s." There is a need for greater emphasis on space-related matters, starting at the highest levels of government.

> *National security space management and organization today fail to reflect the growing importance of space to U.S. interests.*

A. Criteria

In light of the vital place space has in the spectrum of national security interests, a successful approach to organization and management for the future must:

- Provide for national-level guidance that establishes space activity as a fundamental national interest of the United States.

- Create a process to ensure that national-level policy guidance is carried out among and within the relevant agencies and departments.

- Ensure the government's ability to participate effectively in shaping the domestic and international rules and policies that will govern space.

- Create conditions that encourage the Department of Defense to develop and deploy systems in space to deter attack on and, if deterrence should fail, to defend U.S. interests on earth and in space.

- Create conditions that encourage the Intelligence Community to develop revolutionary methods for collecting intelligence from space.

- Provide methods for resolving the inevitable issues between the defense and intelligence sectors on the priority, funding and control of space programs.

Organizing and Managing for the Future

- Account for the increasingly important role played by the commercial and civil space sectors in the nation's domestic and global economic and national security affairs.

- Develop a military and civilian cadre of space professionals within DoD, the Intelligence Community and throughout government more generally.

- Provide an organizational and management structure that permits officials to be agile in addressing the opportunities, risks and threats that inevitably will arise.

- Ensure that DoD and the Intelligence Community are full participants in preparing government positions for international negotiations that may affect U.S. space activities.

B. Assessment of Congressionally Directed Approaches

The Commission was specifically directed by Congress to assess four organizational approaches the Department of Defense might implement for organizing and managing national security space activities. Each is discussed below.

1. A New Military Department for Space

A department is the traditional approach to creating a military organization with responsibility to organize, train and equip forces for operations in a defined medium of activity. Hence, the U.S. today has military departments with the primary missions of providing forces for conducting operations in the air, on land and at sea. The use of space in defense of U.S. interests may require the creation of a military department for space at some future date. A Space Department would provide strong advocacy for space and a single organization with the primary mission of providing forces for conducting both military and intelligence space operations. However, the Commission believes that the disadvantages of creating a department today outweigh the advantages for a number of reasons, including that there is not yet a critical mass of qualified personnel, budget, requirements or missions sufficient to establish a new department. Meanwhile, near- and mid-term organizational adjustments should be fashioned so as to not preclude eventual evolution toward a Space Department if that proves desirable.

2. Space Corps

A Space Corps within the Department of the Air Force may be an appropriate model in its own right or a useful way station in the evolution toward a Space Department. One model is the Army Air Force's relationship to the Army during World War II. Existing Air Force space forces, facilities, units and personnel, and military space missions could be transferred to a Corps. A Space Corps could have authority for acquisition and operation of space systems, perhaps to include both DoD and Intelligence Community systems, while leveraging existing Air Force logistics and support functions. Alternative approaches might be modeled after the relationship of the Marine Corps to the Department of the Navy. A Space Corps would have many of the same advantages and disadvantages of a Space Department. However, unlike a Space Department, a Corps within the Air Force would not eliminate the competition for resources between air and space platforms that exists within the Air Force today. Nor would it by itself alleviate the concerns of other Services and agencies over Air Force space resource allocations.

3. Assistant Secretary of Defense for Space

An Assistant Secretary of Defense for Space reporting to the Secretary of Defense could be created with primary responsibility for space policy. The Commission believes that this position likely would not have sufficient influence over the evolution of U.S. national security space capabilities. Oversight of space policy needs to be coordinated with acquisition and technology development and with command and control, intelligence, and information operations in support of military operations. These activities are now highly integrated. The Commission believes that singling out policy for special treatment by an Assistant Secretary is not likely to result in greater or more effective focus on space within DoD.

An alternative is to position an Assistant Secretary of Defense for Space within the office of the Under Secretary of Defense for Policy and to broaden the scope of responsibilities to include intelligence and information operations. Under this arrangement, the Assistant Secretary for Space would focus on establishing policy guidance for the Department on space, intelligence and information operations, coordinating that policy with the Intelligence Community and acting as DoD's representative for space-related matters in interagency and international fora. This approach would be effective only if a companion office with responsibility for

Organizing and Managing for the Future

oversight of acquisition programs for space, intelligence, information and command, control and communication is assigned to the Under Secretary of Defense for Acquisition, Technology and Logistics. This approach may be better associated with the creation of a Space Department or Space Corps, either of which would presuppose greater focus within DoD on space capabilities. The Commission recommends an alternative arrangement, an Under Secretary of Defense for Space, Intelligence and Information, as described later in this chapter.

4. Major Force Program

A Major Force Program is a Department of Defense mechanism to aggregate related budget items into a single program in order to track program resources independent of the appropriation process. As a management tool, this could be useful in helping make the various elements of the Department's space program more visible and in providing accountability for space funding decisions.

C. Recommendations: A New Approach to Space Organization and Management

The Congress also directed the Commission to consider any other changes to national security space organization and management. The Commission believes that a new and more comprehensive approach is needed to further the nation's security interests in space.

Following are the Commission's unanimous recommendations:

1. Presidential Leadership

The United States has a vital national interest in space. National security space should be high among the nation's priorities. It deserves the attention of the national leadership, from the President down.

> ***The President should consider establishing space as a national security priority.***

Only the President can impress upon the members of the Cabinet, particularly the Secretary of Defense and the Director of Central Intelligence, the priority to be placed on the success of the national space program. To establish a priority on space, the President could direct a review of national space policy. That policy should give the departments and agencies guidance to reflect the national space priorities in building their budgets and programs. The National Security Council can assist the President with measures to monitor the progress of the national space program toward defined goals. This information is useful to the President and Cabinet officials in holding their departments and agencies accountable for achieving the national goals.

2. Presidential Space Advisory Group

The President might find it useful to have access to high-level advice in developing a long-term strategy for sustaining the nation's role as the leading space-faring nation.

> ***The President should consider the appointment of a Presidential Space Advisory Group to provide independent advice on developing and employing new space capabilities.***

A top-level Presidential space advisory group could provide independent advice on new concepts for employing space capabilities for intelligence collection and operations, military operations or commercial advantage (Figure 29). It should be unconstrained in scope and provide

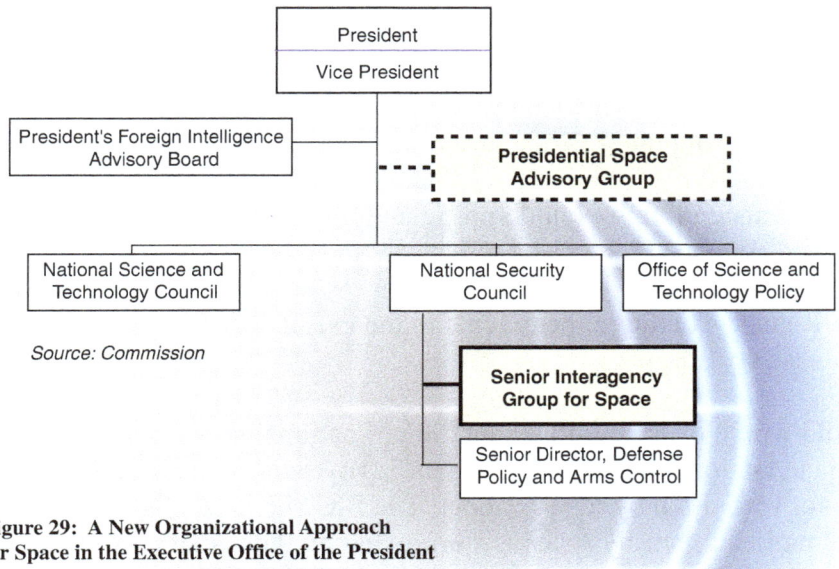

Figure 29: A New Organizational Approach for Space in the Executive Office of the President

recommendations that enable the nation to capitalize on its investment in people, technology, infrastructure and capabilities in all space sectors, to assure that the U.S. sustains its leadership role. The group should seek to identify new technical opportunities that could advance U.S. interests in space. The group should be chartered with a mandate to expire after three years.

3. Senior Interagency Group for Space

The current interagency process is inadequate to address the number, range and complexity of today's space issues, which are expected to increase over time. A standing interagency coordination process is needed to focus on policy formulation and coordination of space activities pertinent to national security and to assure that representation in domestic and international fora effectively reflects U.S. national security and other space interests.

> **The President should direct that a Senior Interagency Group for Space be established and staffed within the National Security Council structure.**

The core membership for a Senior Interagency Group (SIG) for Space should ensure that senior-level attention is directed to specific national security space issues. However, the membership could be expanded to include officials from other relevant departments and agencies as issues warrant.

The central objectives of the interagency process for space should be to:

- Leverage the collective investments in the commercial, civil, defense and intelligence sectors to advance U.S. capabilities in each.

- Advance initiatives in domestic and international fora that preserve and enhance U.S. use of and access to space.

- Reduce existing impediments to the use of space for national security purposes.

The SIG would oversee implementation of national space policy, coordinate national security space matters government-wide and frame key issues for resolution by the President. The SIG should focus on the most critical national security space issues, including those that span the civil and commercial space sectors. Its agenda might include:

- Space control.

- Military missions in space.

- Space transportation.

- Space utilities, including GPS, weather, rescue, space surveillance, spectrum and communications.

- Earth remote sensing.

- Domestic, allied and international agreement, treaty and regulatory regimes.

The agenda should be shaped to produce a deliberate, coherent approach to the implementation of space policy. To develop the group's agenda and to coordinate national security space matters at the working level, the Senior Interagency Group would need dedicated staff support, provided through the National Security Council staff, with experience across the four space sectors.

4. SecDef/DCI Relationship

The issues relating to space between the Department of Defense and the Intelligence Community are sufficiently numerous and complex that their successful resolution and implementation require a close, continuing and effective relationship between the Secretary of Defense and the Director of Central Intelligence.

> **The Secretary of Defense and the Director of Central Intelligence should meet regularly to address national security space policy, objectives and issues.**

5. Under Secretary of Defense for Space, Intelligence and Information

Until space organizations have more fully evolved, the Office of the Secretary of Defense would benefit from having a senior-level official with sufficient standing to serve as the advocate for space within the Department. The Secretary of Defense would assign this official responsibility to oversee the Department's research and development, acquisition, launch and operation of its space, intelligence and information assets; coordinate the military intelligence activities within the Department; and work with the Intelligence Community on long-range intelligence requirements for national security.

An Under Secretary of Defense for Space, Intelligence and Information should be established.

An Under Secretary of Defense for Space, Intelligence and Information (USD (SII)) would provide policy, guidance and oversight for space in a single organization within the Office of the Secretary of Defense (Figure 30). The USD (SII) would help ensure that space-related issues are addressed in the Department at an appropriately influential level. This is particularly important in the near term to help advance the development of new space missions and associated forces.

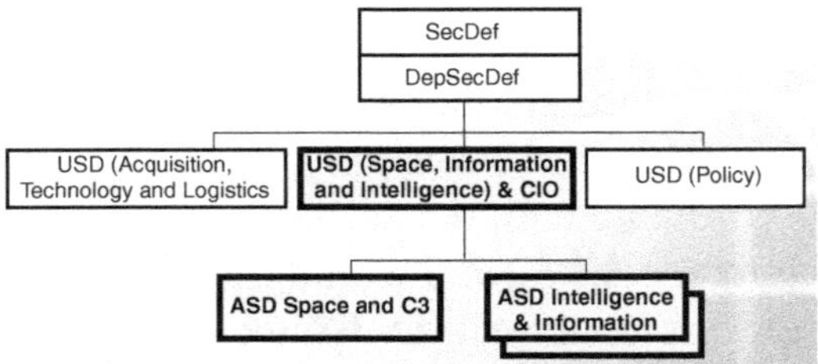

Figure 30: A New Organizational Approach for Space in the Office of the Secretary of Defense

Source: Commission

The Under Secretary would absorb the responsibilities of the current ASD (C3I) and would serve as the senior OSD advocate for space. This might require a change in the legislation establishing the office of the ASD (C3I). The USD (SII) would provide policy recommendations to the Secretary of Defense for the future course and direction for space activity within the Department of Defense. An Under Secretary would have the rank to work effectively with the military Services and with the CINCs and Joint Staff. This organization would also provide more senior-level attention to intelligence and information operations, particularly as they relate to establishing longer-term space-related policies. This can be done by assigning space and C3 acquisition-related issues to one Assistant Secretary of Defense. A second Assistant Secretary could be assigned responsibility for intelligence and information. The Under Secretary would represent the Department within the interagency process on all but matters of high national policy, up to the level of the Deputies' committees.

The Under Secretary, on behalf of the Secretary of Defense, would be assigned responsibility to:

- Establish space policy in coordination with the Under Secretary of Defense for Policy and oversee space system acquisition in coordination with the Under Secretary of Defense for Acquisition, Technology and Logistics.

- Implement policy to enable deployment and employment of space assets to conduct new military missions in the areas of space protection and projecting force in and from space.

- Oversee research and development, acquisition, launch and operation of space, intelligence and information assets and ensure that they are considered in an end-to-end fashion.

- On behalf of the Secretary of Defense, coordinate military intelligence activities within the Department and work with the Intelligence Community on long-range intelligence requirements for national security.

- Coordinate DoD space activities with the commercial and civil sectors at home and abroad.

- Develop the still nascent field of information assurance and information operations by defining the mission area, coordinating efforts within the Department and coordinating departmental plans with those in the broader government community.

- Fulfill the role of Chief Information Officer as provided in Title 44 U.S.C.

- Oversee the Department's information architecture.

6. Commander in Chief of U.S. Space Command and NORAD and Commander, Air Force Space Command

The Commander in Chief, U.S. Space Command should continue to concentrate on space as it relates to warfare in the mediums of air, land and sea, as well as space. His primary role is to conduct space operations and provide space-related services, to include computer network defense/

Organizing and Managing for the Future

attack missions in support of the operations of the other CINCs, and national missile defense. This broad and varied set of responsibilities as CINCSPACE will leave less time for his other assigned duties.

> **The Secretary of the Air Force should assign responsibility for the command of Air Force Space Command to a four-star officer other than CINCSPACE/CINCNORAD.**
>
> **The Secretary of Defense should end the practice of assigning only Air Force flight-rated officers to the position of CINCSPACE and CINCNORAD to ensure that an officer from any Service with an understanding of combat and space could be assigned to this position.**

In today's arrangement, CINCSPACE also serves as CINCNORAD and Commander of Air Force Space Command. Current practice assigns a rated pilot as CINCNORAD, though the actual requirement is that the NORAD Director of Operations, a J-3 position, be flight rated. As a result, only flight-rated U.S. Air Force officers serve as CINCSPACE and CINCNORAD.

To let the best-qualified officer from any Service fill the position of CINCSPACE, the Department should end the practice of assigning only flight-rated officers as CINCNORAD and end the practice of assigning CINCSPACE to serve also as Commander, Air Force Space Command. This would help ensure that an officer from any Service with an understanding of combat and space could be assigned as CINCSPACE, and one with the required in-depth knowledge of space acquisition and operations could be made Commander, Air Force Space Command. The Commission believes that the position of CINCSPACE should remain nominative and need not be rotated among the military Services.

Freed of the role as Commander, Air Force Space Command and the associated responsibilities devoted to the needs of a single Service, CINCSPACE would be better positioned to play a significant role in developing long-term requirements for space systems for the Department as a whole, which are increasingly "joint."

There is no need to establish a specific set of experience requirements for CINCSPACE. As space education, career development and training in the Department of Defense are enriched, a cadre of space professionals will develop. A larger pool of senior officers will emerge with knowledge of space and experience in combat operations, providing a rich pool of leadership and operational experience from which to draw the country's most senior space commanders, among them CINCSPACE.

The Commission is also concerned about the short tenure among individuals serving as CINCSPACE and in other senior space positions, particularly as many of these individuals do not, today, come to the jobs with extensive space experience. While national security space missions evolve and mature, it would be useful for an individual to remain in this position for a period beyond the typical two-year commitment. With a longer time horizon, CINCSPACE could establish appropriate goals and objectives for maturing space missions and remain long enough to shape their development.

7. Military Services

The Department of Defense requires space systems that can be employed in independent operations or in support of air, land and sea forces to deter and defend against hostile actions directed at the interests of the United States. In the mid term, a Space Corps within the Air Force may be appropriate to meet this requirement; in the longer term, it may be met by a military department for space. In the nearer term, a realigned, rechartered Air Force is best suited to organize, train and equip space forces.

> **The Air Force should realign headquarters and field commands to more effectively organize, train and equip for prompt and sustained space operations. Air Force Space Command (AFSPC) should be assigned responsibility for providing the resources to execute space research, development, acquisition and operations, under the command of a four-star general. The Army and Navy would still establish requirements and develop and deploy space systems unique to each Service.**

> **Amend Title 10 U.S.C. to assign the Air Force responsibility to organize, train and equip for prompt and sustained offensive and defensive air _and_ space operations. In addition, the Secretary of Defense should designate the Air Force as Executive Agent for Space within the Department of Defense.**

Organizing and Managing for the Future

To carry out this realignment, Space and Missile Systems Center, now under the Air Force Materiel Command, would be reassigned to Air Force Space Command. The Commander, AFSPC would have authority to program funds and direct research and development programs within the Air Force laboratory system (Figure 31).

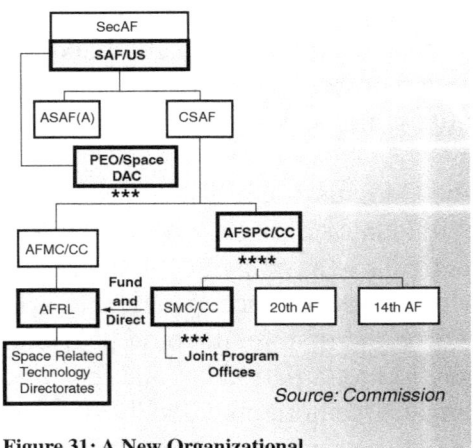

Figure 31: A New Organizational Approach for Space in the Air Force

Consolidating space functions into a single organization would create a strong center of advocacy for space and an environment in which to develop a cadre of space professionals. This cadre should be charged with developing doctrine, concepts of operations and new systems to achieve national space goals and objectives. The arrangement would increase the role of the uniformed military in research, development and acquisition of space systems to better meet operational requirements.

Air Force Space Command would become the center for developing a space cadre and advocating education and training programs for space professionals. The commander should have responsibility for managing all aspects of the space career field, to include developing new space career paths and defining and implementing selection and assignment criteria.

8. Aligning Air Force and NRO Space Programs

The Department of Defense and the Intelligence Community would benefit from the appointment of a single official within the Air Force with authority for the acquisition of space systems for the Air Force and the NRO based on the "best practices" of each organization.

> **Assign the Under Secretary of the Air Force as the Director of the National Reconnaissance Office. Designate the Under Secretary as the Air Force Acquisition Executive for Space.**

Organizing and Managing for the Future

This appointment would require a decision by the Secretary of Defense with the concurrence of the Director of Central Intelligence. It would serve several purposes. It would create a senior-level advocate for space within the Air Force. It would give a single person authority to acquire space systems for the Air Force and the NRO. Space would be strongly represented in the planning, programming and budgeting process and in the defense acquisition process. The Under Secretary would oversee space matters related to acquisition, financial management, manpower and infrastructure.

This would better align Service and NRO space acquisition organizations and would provide an opportunity to align space acquisition policies with the "best practices" of each. It would also help the Under Secretary in his current role in the Air Force resource process to ensure balance between air and space programs within the Air Force.

Designating the Air Force Under Secretary/DNRO as the acquisition executive for space would require a change in DoD directives, and there might be a need for Congressional action to amend Title 10 U.S.C. Currently, both the directives and the law imply that a Service may have only a single acquisition executive.

Additional organizational changes would be required in the Air Force as well. The position of the Assistant Secretary of the Air Force for Space would be eliminated. The staff functions performed by the Deputy Assistant Secretary of the Air Force for Space Plans and Policy would be transferred to the Under Secretary of the Air Force. To support the realignment of Air Force space acquisition responsibilities, the Program Executive Officer for Space, the Designated Acquisition Commander and the Director of Space and Nuclear Deterrence would also be re-assigned directly to the Under Secretary of the Air Force to provide program oversight and staff support for Air Force space acquisition programs.

In this new position, the Under Secretary/DNRO, in consultation with the Secretary of Defense and DCI, would select and oversee the National Security Space Architect. The Architect would be responsible for end-to-end architectures for all national security space systems, including user terminals, which would continue to be acquired within the individual Services. This places the architecture function within the resource processes of both the Air Force and the NRO, which should make it more effective. The National Security Space Architect would also be responsible for ensuring that NRO and Air Force program funding for space is consistent with policy, planning guidance and architectural decisions.

A flag officer of any Service or a senior civilian could fill the position of architect. The office would remain jointly staffed by the Intelligence Community and the military Services. Currently the NSSA has five joint billets—one Navy, two Army and two Air Force. The Commission recommends that each NSSA military position be designated as a "joint position" to encourage further participation by all the Services in this activity.

Meeting Army and Navy Requirements

The changes described, to realign Air Force space activities and align Air Force/NRO space activities, would elevate space within DoD and better position the Air Force to provide for the Department's needs for space doctrine and programs. An important Air Force responsibility is to ensure that the requirements and equities of the other military Services for space systems and capabilities are met as well. This would be accomplished in a number of ways. The Army and Navy would provide appropriately qualified officers to joint commands and agencies, including the NRO, to ensure that these agencies and commands have staff qualified to understand and meet joint requirements for space systems and products. These would include U.S. Space Command and the office of the National Security Space Architect.

The practice of acquiring most space systems through joint program offices would be continued and encouraged. The Army and Navy would need to develop, deploy, fund and, where appropriate, operate space systems to meet unique requirements. This would require the Army and Navy to maintain a cadre of space-qualified officers to represent their interests in space requirements, acquisition and operations.

Implementation

There are several possible ways to provide formal authorities to the Air Force for this new organization. One is to give the Air Force statutory responsibility under Title 10 U.S.C. to "organize, train and equip" for space, which the Commission recommends. Currently, the Air Force "shall be organized, trained, and equipped primarily for prompt and sustained offensive and defensive air operations." This could be changed to "air and space operations." It would establish a Congressionally mandated obligation for the Air Force to plan, program and budget for space missions. This approach should motivate the Air Force to give space activities higher priority.

The Commission recommends the Secretary of Defense designate the Air Force formally as the Executive Agent for Space, with department-wide responsibility for planning, programming and acquisition of space systems.

Organizing and Managing for the Future

In this role, the Air Force would be responsible for developing, defending and submitting a joint "Space Program Plan" to the Office of the Secretary of Defense. The Army and Navy would continue to develop and fund space programs that meet their unique requirements and would submit them to the Executive Agent for inclusion in the joint space program. The Services would continue to acquire Service-specific programs but, for these, would report through the Air Force Space Acquisition Executive. The Services would continue to develop requirements through the Joint Requirements Oversight Council process, but under this arrangement the Executive Agent would harmonize the requirements with plans, programs and budgets before submission. The Services would retain responsibility for doctrine, strategy, education, training and operations, but in coordination with the Executive Agent.

The recommended realignment of space activities within the Air Force would create a single chain of authority from the Under Secretary of the Air Force through both the Air Force space organizations and the NRO. It would give the Air Force a clear opportunity to create a space-oriented culture comprised of military professionals who could directly influence the development of systems and doctrine for use in space operations.

The nation's vital interests depend increasingly on the capability of its military professionals to develop, acquire and operate systems capable of sustained space combat operations. The proliferation of technology and the ease with which hostile entities can gain access to space increase the need for a concentrated effort to deter and defend against such attacks.

Such efforts are not being pursued with the vision and attention needed. U.S. interests in space may well ultimately call for the creation of a Space Corps or a Space Department to organize, train and equip forces for sustained operations in space. For that reason, assignment of Title 10 responsibility to the Air Force by the Congress and its designation as Executive Agent for Space within the Department of Defense is recommended to lay the foundation for such future steps.

Future Steps

> *The Commission believes that once the realignment in the Air Force is complete, a logical step toward a Space Department could be to transition from the new Air Force Space Command to a Space Corps within the Air Force.*

Organizing and Managing for the Future

This would be, in essence, an evolution much like that of the Army's air forces from the Army Air Corps, into the Army Air Forces and eventually into the Department of the Air Force. The timetable, which is not possible to predict, would be dictated by circumstances over the next five to ten years.

The likelihood of independent operations in space will grow as ballistic missile defense, space control and information operations are integrated into the contingency plans of theater commanders. Much as theater commanders now employ air, land or sea forces, space forces can either perform independent operations unique to their medium or capabilities or be used as part of a joint force. A Space Corps could develop forces, doctrine and concepts of operation for space systems for use as a functional component of a theater commander's order of battle.

The Commander, Air Force Space Command would serve as head of a Space Corps and could join the deliberations of the Joint Chiefs of Staff when space-related issues are on the agenda. The Corps would have responsibility for planning, programming and budgeting for space systems. It could be possible, however, for DoD to transition directly to a Space Department if future conditions support that step more quickly than appears likely from the Commission's vantage point today.

> *Finally, an evolution to a Space Corps could involve integration of the Air Force and NRO acquisition and operations activities for space systems.*

This integration could be achieved either by merging the two organizations in one step or through a series of steps in an evolution to a Space Corps or a Space Department. The Commission believes that a series of steps will likely prove to be the most appropriate path. Toward that end, when practicable after the realignment in the Air Force, the Commission recommends:

- Acquisition of the NRO's next generation communications relay satellite be transferred to the Air Force.

- Responsibility for operation of the NRO's satellites be transferred by the Secretary of Defense and the Director of Central Intelligence to the realigned Air Force.

- The NRO and Air Force activities be fully merged, creating a single organization responsible for the development, acquisition and operation of the nation's space-based defense and intelligence systems.

- For programs transferred from the NRO, program execution would continue with existing acquisition authorities within the DoD structure; guidance for requirements, priorities and resources would continue to be provided by the Director of Central Intelligence. These programs would continue to be funded in the National Reconnaissance Program as part of the National Foreign Intelligence Program.

9. Innovative Research and Development

The Intelligence Community has a need for revolutionary methods, including but not limited to space systems, for collecting intelligence.

The Secretary of Defense and the Director of Central Intelligence should direct the creation of a research, development and demonstration organization to focus on this requirement.

Intelligence collection from space continues to be made increasingly difficult by greater target complexity, greater capabilities to deceive and deny U.S. space-based assets and greater demands on the system. The Intelligence Community is being asked to provide a larger volume of information and more particular types of products, especially with respect to scientific and technical intelligence.

Space systems now deployed and in development by the NRO require a considerable period of time to develop, are expensive to acquire and to place on orbit, have low operation and maintenance costs and have lifetimes stretching to nearly a decade. Many users in the Intelligence Community and the Department of Defense now rely on high quality intelligence products available on call. As a result, the NRO's requirements and acquisition processes favor conservative technical and system solutions to intelligence and military requirements. Combined with the reality of budget constraints, the result is that relatively less emphasis is placed on research, development and demonstration of new concepts and capabilities to satisfy critical intelligence needs.

A Strategic Reconnaissance Office would focus on the unique, one- or two-of-a-kind systems needed to address an urgent national requirement. It would retain control over the systems through acquisition and operational deployment. It should be operated as a joint venture between the Secretary of Defense and the Director of Central Intelligence. It should be relatively small in size and staffed by highly motivated people with the means to move a project rapidly from concept to deployed system. The budget would be contained within the NFIP, but outside the NRP. In developing systems, the office would not be limited to space solutions, but rather it could consider tradeoffs among air, space, surface and subsurface alternatives.

Competitive centers of innovation that actively pursue space-related research, development and demonstration programs are desirable.

> **The Secretary of Defense should direct the Defense Advanced Research Projects Agency and the Services' laboratories to undertake development and demonstration of innovative space technologies and systems for dedicated military missions.**

DARPA should fund exploratory research and development and demonstration projects that exploit existing technology or apply new technology to existing or emerging requirements. These could be conducted on a classified or unclassified basis, depending on the sensitivity of the technology, mission or operational concept.

The Departments of the Army and Navy should increase and fortify their investments in and execution of research and development programs with emphasis on the uses of space to carry out their respective missions. This would not only ensure multiple sources of innovation, but also would help the Army and Navy retain a space-qualified cadre of engineers and scientists who could represent the individual Services' interests in space requirements, acquisition and operations.

10. Budgeting for Space

Better visibility into the level and distribution of fiscal and personnel resources would improve management and oversight of space programs.

> **The Secretary of Defense should establish a Major Force Program for Space.**

Organizing and Managing for the Future

A Major Force Program for Space should be managed in a decentralized fashion similar to Major Force Programs 1 through 10. The MFP would contain the same program elements as the previously recommended Space Program Plan, which is under the direction of the Air Force as Executive Agent for Space.

If properly highlighted, the current DoD program, budget and accounting information system is adequate to identify and track programs of management interest. A Major Force Program for Space would provide insight into the management of space programs without unnecessarily restricting the flexibility of the Secretary of Defense, the Director of Central Intelligence or the military departments.

Resources for Space Capabilities

Looking to the future, the Department of Defense will undertake new responsibilities in space, including deterrence and defense of space-based assets as well as other defense and power projection missions in and from space. These new missions will require development of new systems and capabilities.

Space capabilities are not funded at a level commensurate with their relative importance. Nor is there a plan in place to build up to the investments needed to modernize existing systems and procure new capabilities. Notionally, investments devoted to the buildup of strategic forces in the 1960s averaged some ten percent of the Department's budget annually. Appropriate investments in space-based capabilities would enable the Department to pursue:

- Improved space situational awareness and attack warning capabilities.

- Enhanced protection/defensive measures, prevention and negation systems and rapid long-range power projection capabilities.

- Modernized launch capabilities.

- A more robust science and technology program for developing and deploying space-based radar, space-based laser, hyper-spectral sensors and reusable launch vehicle technology.

Providing the Department of Defense and the Intelligence Community with additional resources to accomplish these new missions should be considered as part of U.S. national space policy.

11. Congress

Congress is concerned about the organization and management of national security space activities. It will play a key role in reviewing and coordinating many of the recommendations in this report and in helping promote a greater public understanding of the importance of national security space.

This report offers suggestions for organizational changes in the executive branch that are intended to bring a more focused, well-directed approach to the conduct of national security space activities, based on a clear national space policy directed by the President. These organizational changes in the executive branch suggest changes in the Congressional committee and subcommittee structure to align the jurisdictions of these committees as much as possible with the executive branch, leading to a more streamlined process. Congress might usefully consider encouraging greater "crossover" membership among all of the space-related committees to increase legislative coordination among defense and intelligence space programs.

The Commission believes that its recommendations, taken as a whole, will enable the U.S. to sustain its position as the world's leading space-faring nation. Presidential leadership and guidance, coupled with a more effective interagency process and especially with improved coordination between the Department of Defense and the Intelligence Community, are essential if the nation is to promote and protect its interests in space.

VII. Conclusions of the Commission

The members of this Commission have, together, identified five matters of key importance that we believe need attention quickly from the top levels of the U.S. Government. We have drawn these conclusions from six months of assessing U.S. national security space activities, including 32 days of meetings with 77 present and former senior officials and knowledgeable private sector representatives. These five matters—our unanimous conclusions—are:

> **First, the present extent of U.S. dependence on space, the rapid pace at which this dependence is increasing and the vulnerabilities it creates, all demand that U.S. national security space interests be recognized as a top national security priority. The only way they will receive this priority is through specific guidance and direction from the very highest government levels. Only the President has the authority, first, to set forth the national space policy, and then to provide the guidance and direction to senior officials, that together are needed to ensure that the United States remains the world's leading space-faring nation. Only Presidential leadership can ensure the cooperation needed from all space sectors—commercial, civil, defense and intelligence.**

> **Second, the U.S. Government—in particular, the Department of Defense and the Intelligence Community—is not yet arranged or focused to meet the national security space needs of the 21st century. Our growing dependence on space, our vulnerabilities in space and the burgeoning opportunities from space are simply not reflected in the present institutional arrangements. After examining a variety of organizational approaches, the Commission concluded that a number of disparate space activities should promptly be merged, chains of command adjusted, lines of communication opened and policies modified to achieve greater responsibility and accountability. Only then can the necessary trade-offs be made, the appropriate priorities be established and the opportunities for improving U.S. military and intelligence capabilities be realized. Only with senior-level leadership, when properly managed and with the right priorities, will U.S. space programs both deserve and attract the funding that is required.**

Conclusions of the Commission

Third, U.S. national security space programs are vital to peace and stability, and the two officials primarily responsible and accountable for those programs are the Secretary of Defense and the Director of Central Intelligence. Their relationship is critical to the development and deployment of the space capabilities needed to support the President in war, in crisis and also in peace. They must work closely and effectively together, in partnership, both to set and maintain the course for national security space programs and to resolve the differences that arise between their respective bureaucracies. Only if they do so will the armed forces, the Intelligence Community and the National Command Authorities have the information they need to pursue our deterrence and defense objectives successfully in this complex, changing and still dangerous world.

Fourth, we know from history that every medium—air, land and sea—has seen conflict. Reality indicates that space will be no different. Given this virtual certainty, the U.S. must develop the means both to deter and to defend against hostile acts in and from space. This will require superior space capabilities. Thus far, the broad outline of U.S. national space policy is sound, but the U.S. has not yet taken the steps necessary to develop the needed capabilities and to maintain and ensure continuing superiority.

Finally, investment in science and technology resources—not just facilities, but people—is essential if the U.S. is to remain the world's leading space-faring nation. The U.S. Government needs to play an active, deliberate role in expanding and deepening the pool of military and civilian talent in science, engineering and systems operations that the nation will need. The government also needs to sustain its investment in enabling and breakthrough technologies in order to maintain its leadership in space.

Attachment A

Résumés of Commission Members

The Honorable Duane P. Andrews

Mr. Andrews is Corporate Executive Vice President and Director, Science Applications International Corporation (SAIC) (1993 to present). He previously was an officer in the United States Air Force (1967-77), a professional staff member with the House Permanent Select Committee on Intelligence (1977-89), and the Assistant Secretary of Defense for Command, Control, Communications and Intelligence (1989-93). Mr. Andrews was awarded the Department of Defense Medal for Distinguished Public Service and the National Intelligence Distinguished Service Medal.

Mr. Robert V. Davis

Mr. Davis is President of R.V. Davis & Associates (1997 to present). He previously was a professional staff member of the House Appropriations Committee (1977-95) and Deputy Under Secretary of Defense for Space (1995-97). Mr. Davis was awarded the Secretary of Defense Medal for Outstanding Public Service (1997).

General Howell M. Estes, III, United States Air Force (Retired)

General Estes is President of Howell Estes & Associates, Inc. (1998 to present) and serves as Vice Chairman of the Board of Trustees, The Aerospace Corporation. He entered the United States Air Force in 1965 and served for 33 years. At the time of his retirement in 1998, General Estes was Commander in Chief, North American Aerospace Defense Command, Commander in Chief, United States Space Command, and Commander, Air Force Space Command. He previously served as a consultant to the Defense Science Board Task Force on Space Superiority (1999).

General Ronald R. Fogleman, United States Air Force (Retired)

General Fogleman is president and chief operating officer of the B Bar J Cattle and Consulting Company, Durango Aerospace Incorporated, and a partner in Laird and Company, LLC (1998 to present). He entered the United States Air Force in 1963 and served for 34 years. At the time of his retirement in 1997, General Fogleman was Chief of Staff of the U.S. Air Force. He previously served as the Commander in Chief of the U.S. Transportation Command (1992-94). He serves on the Boards of Directors for International Airline Service Group, DERCO Aerospace, EAST Inc., Mesa Air Group, MITRE Corporation, North American Airlines, Rolls-Royce North America, and World Airways. General Fogleman is a member of the Council on Foreign Relations.

Lieutenant General Jay M. Garner, United States Army (Retired)

General Garner is President of SY Technology (1997 to present). He entered the United States Army in 1962 and served for 35 years. Prior to leaving military service in 1997, he served as Assistant Vice Chief of Staff of the Army (1996-97). Previously he was the Commander of the U.S. Army Space and Strategic Defense Command (1994-96).

The Honorable William R. Graham

Dr. Graham is the Chairman of the Board and President of National Security Research, Inc. (1997 to present). He previously served as the Deputy Administrator of the National Aeronautics and Space Administration (1985-86), Science Advisor to President Reagan and Director of the White House Office of Science & Technology Policy (1986-89), and Member of the Commission to Assess the Ballistic Missile Threat to the United States (1998). He has a Ph.D. in electrical engineering.

General Charles A. Horner, United States Air Force (Retired)

General Horner is a business consultant, author and national defense advisor (1994 to present). He entered the United States Air Force in 1958 and served for 36 years. He served as Commander in Chief, North American Aerospace Defense Command, Commander in Chief, United States Space Command, Commander, Air Force Space Command, and he commanded Allied Air Forces during the 1991 Gulf War.

Admiral David E. Jeremiah, United States Navy (Retired)

Admiral Jeremiah is President of Technology Strategies & Alliances Corporation (1994 to present). Prior to leaving military service in 1994, he served as Vice Chairman, Joint Chiefs of Staff (1990-94) for Generals Powell and Shalikashvili. He serves on the Boards of Directors for several firms, including Litton Industries, Alliant Techsystems Inc., Getronics Government Systems, LLC and Geobiotics, Inc. Admiral Jeremiah serves on various national security and intelligence panels, boards and commissions, including the Defense Policy Board, and a National Reconnaissance Office Advisory Panel.

General Thomas S. Moorman, Jr., United States Air Force (Retired)

General Moorman is a Partner in Booz-Allen Hamilton (1998 to present). He also serves as a member of the Board of Trustees for The Aerospace Corporation, is an Outside Director on the Board of Smiths Industries and is a member of the Defense Policy Board Advisory Committee. He entered the United States Air Force in 1962 and served for 35 years. General Moorman served as Commander of Air Force Space Command (1990-92). At the time of his retirement in 1997, General Moorman was Vice Chief of Staff, United States Air Force. He is a member of the Council on Foreign Relations.

Mr. Douglas H. Necessary

Mr. Necessary is an independent management consultant. He has recently served on several government boards. He served on active duty in the U.S. Army from 1964-1984 and as a professional staff member of the Committee on Armed Services, U.S. House of Representatives (1984-2000).

General Glenn K. Otis, United States Army (Retired)

General Otis serves as a consultant for many defense firms and serves on the Defense Science Board and Ballistic Missile Defense Advisory Committee. Previously he was Senior Vice President of Coleman Research Corporation (1988-96) and Chairman of the Board on Army Science and Technology at the National Academy of Sciences. He entered the United States Army in 1946 and served for 42 years. Prior to leaving military service in 1988, he served as Commander in Chief, U.S. Army Europe and 7th Army, and Commander, NATO's Central Army Group (1983-88). Previously he commanded the U.S. Army's Training and Doctrine Command (1981-83).

The Honorable Donald H. Rumsfeld*

Mr. Rumsfeld is currently in private business. He serves as Chairman of the Board of Directors of Gilead Sciences, Inc., and on the Boards of Directors of a number of corporations and non-profit organizations. Previously he served as CEO of G.D. Searle & Co. and of General Instruments Corporation, and in a variety of U.S. government posts, including: Naval Aviator, Member of U.S. Congress, U.S. Ambassador to NATO, White House Chief of Staff, Secretary of Defense, Presidential Envoy to the Middle East and Chairman of the Commission to Assess the Ballistic Missile Threat to the United States. He received the Presidential Medal of Freedom, the nation's highest civilian award, in 1977.

Senator Malcolm Wallop (Retired)

Senator Wallop is currently a Senior Fellow with the Heritage Foundation and chairs Frontiers of Freedom, a non-profit public policy organization he established in January 1995. Previously he served as a U.S. Senator from Wyoming (1977-95). In 1977 he was the first elected official to propose a space-based missile defense system. Prior to serving in the U.S. Senate, he was a rancher, a businessman, and a member of the Wyoming Legislature (1969-76).

---

* The Honorable Donald H. Rumsfeld served as a member and chairman of the Commission from its inception until December 28, 2000, when he was nominated for the position of Secretary of Defense by President-elect George W. Bush.

Attachment B

Résumés of Core Staff of the Commission

Dr. Stephen A. Cambone, Staff Director. Research Director, Institute for National Strategic Studies, National Defense University (1998 to present). Staff Director, Commission to Assess the Ballistic Missile Threat to the United States (1998); Senior Fellow, Center for Strategic and International Studies (1993-98); Director, Strategic Defense Policy, Office of the Secretary of Defense (1990-93); Deputy Director of Strategic Analysis, SRS Technologies (1986-90); Staff Analyst, Los Alamos National Laboratory (1982-86). Ph.D. in political science.

D. Craig Baker, Staff Member. Special Assistant to the Chief Scientist, U.S. Army Space and Missile Defense Command (1999-2000); Concepts and Initiatives Division Chief, Army Space and Missile Defense Battle Lab (1997-98); Plans Director, Army Space Command (1996-97); Space Integration Division Chief, Army Space Command (1990-96); Army Research Fellow, RAND Arroyo Center (1986-88). M.S. in national security strategy. M.S. in systems management.

Barbara Bicksler, Staff Member. Senior Policy Analyst, Strategic Analysis, Inc. (1996 to present). Research Staff Member, Institute for Defense Analyses (1986-95); Analyst, Office of the Assistant Secretary of Defense for Program Analysis and Evaluation (1981-84). Master in Public Policy.

Linda L. Haller, Staff Member. Assistant Bureau Chief (1999 to present) and Senior Legal Advisor (1997-99), International Bureau, Federal Communications Commission (FCC); Senior Counsel, Office of General Counsel, FCC (1994-97); Attorney Advisor, FCC (1991-92); Associate, Morgan Lewis & Bockius (1988-90); Associate, Pierson, Ball & Dowd (1986-88). Juris Doctor.

Delonnie Henry, Staff Member. Committee Clerk, U.S. House Select Committee on U.S. Technology Transfers to the People's Republic of China (1998-99); Commission to Assess the Ballistic Missile Threat to the United States (Rumsfeld Commission) (1998); National Defense University (1993-98). M.Ed.

John Luddy, Staff Member. Senior Policy Advisor, U.S. Senator Jon Kyl (1999-2000); Senior Legislative Assistant, U. S. Senator Bob Smith (1997-99); Military Legislative Assistant, U.S. Senator James Inhofe (1995-97); Defense Policy Analyst, The Heritage Foundation (1992-95); U.S. Marine Corps (1986-89). M.S. in international relations.

Lieutenant Colonel J. Kevin McLaughlin, United States Air Force, Staff Member. Commander, 2d Space Operations Squadron (1998-2000); Chief, Space/Missile Branch, Legislative Liaison (1996-98); Chief, Space Policy, Assistant Secretary of the Air Force (Space) (1995-96); Titan Launch Controller/Deputy for Standards/Evaluation, 45th Space Wing (1991-94). M.A. in space systems management.

William E. Savage, Staff Member. Director of Strategic Development for Space Programs, Litton TASC (1994 to present). National Reconnaissance Office (1986-94); U.S. Air Force Space Program (1967-86). M.S. in astro-geophysics.

G. Randall Seftas, Staff Member. Project Manager/Lead Engineer, National Aeronautics and Space Administration (1994-Present); Senior Research Engineer, Lockheed Missiles and Space Company (1989-94); Spacecraft Systems Engineer, Booz-Allen & Hamilton (1988-89); Operational Space Systems Engineer, GE Space Systems Division (1984-88). B.S. in aerospace engineering.

Thomas L. Wilson, Jr., Staff Member. Deputy Head, Program Coordination and Liaison Office, Naval Center for Space Technology (1997 to present). Program Manager, Naval Research Laboratory (1992-2000). Professional Staff, Office of the Deputy Under Secretary of Defense for Space (1996-98). B.S. in aerospace engineering.

Department of Defense Liaison

Major General H. J. "Mitch" Mitchell, United States Air Force. Department of Defense Liaison to the Commission to Assess United States National Security Space Management and Organization and Special Assistant to the Assistant Secretary of Defense for Command, Control, Communications and Intelligence. Former National Security Space Architect.

Attachment C

Commission Meetings

July 11, 2000

    The Honorable Arthur L. Money — Assistant Secretary of Defense for Command, Control, Communications and Intelligence and DoD Chief Information Officer

July 26, 2000

    The Honorable Porter J. Goss — Co-Chairman, National Commission for the Review of the National Reconnaissance Office and Chairman, Permanent Select Committee on Intelligence, U.S. House of Representatives

    The Honorable J. Robert Kerrey — Co-Chairman, National Commission for the Review of the National Reconnaissance Office and former Vice Chairman, Select Committee on Intelligence, U.S. Senate

    Mr. Ken Colucci — Chief of Staff, National Commission for the Review of the National Reconnaissance Office

    Mr. Art Grant — Executive Staff Director, National Commission for the Review of the National Reconnaissance Office

July 27, 2000

    The Honorable Edward C. "Pete" Aldridge — Chief Executive Officer, The Aerospace Corporation and former Secretary of the Air Force and Director of the National Reconnaissance Office

August 7, 2000

    Mr. Lawrence K. Gershwin — National Intelligence Officer for Science and Technology, National Intelligence Council

    Mr. Marc Berkowitz — Director of Space Policy, Office of the Assistant Secretary of Defense for Command, Control, Communications and Intelligence

August 8, 2000

    LTG John Costello, U.S. Army — Commanding General, U.S. Army Space & Missile Defense Command

    VADM Richard Mayo, USN — Deputy Director, U.S. Navy Space Information Warfare Command & Control

August 23, 2000

LtGen Emil R. Bedard, USMC	Deputy Chief of Staff for Plans, Policies and Operations, Headquarters, U.S. Marine Corps
Maj Gen H. Marshall Ward, USAF	Director, Special Programs, Office of the Under Secretary of Defense for Acquisition, Technology and Logistics
The Honorable Keith Hall	Assistant Secretary of the Air Force for Space and Director of the National Reconnaissance Office
Mr. David A. Kier	Deputy Director, National Reconnaissance Office

August 24, 2000

Mr. Richard L. Shiffrin	Deputy General Counsel (Intelligence), Department of Defense
Mr. W. Harvey Dalton	Associate Deputy General Counsel (International Affairs and Intelligence), Department of Defense
Mr. Richard K. Sylvester	Assistant Deputy Undersecretary of Defense (Systems Acquisition)
The Honorable John Hamre	President and Chief Executive Officer, Center for Strategic and International Studies and former Deputy Secretary of Defense
Mr. James M. Simon, Jr.	Assistant Director of Central Intelligence for Administration
Mr. Larry Kindsvater	Executive Director, Intelligence Community Affairs, Office of the Director of Central Intelligence
Mr. Charles Allen	Assistant Deputy Director of Central Intelligence for Collection, Office of the Director of Central Intelligence
Mr. John Gannon	Assistant Deputy Director of Central Intelligence for Production and Analysis, Office of the Director of Central Intelligence

September 19, 2000

Lt Gen Robert H. Foglesong, USAF	Deputy Chief of Staff for Air and Space Operations
Brig Gen Daniel P. Leaf, USAF	Director of Operational Requirements
Gen Michael E. Ryan, USAF	Chief of Staff, United States Air Force
Maj Gen Brian A. Arnold, USAF	Director of Space and Nuclear Deterrence, Office of the Secretary of the Air Force for Acquisition

The Honorable Arthur L. Money	Assistant Secretary of Defense for Command, Control, Communications and Intelligence and DoD Chief Information Officer
Mr. Kenneth F. Colucci	Chief of Staff, National Commission for the Review of the National Reconnaissance Office
Mr. Arthur V. Grant	Executive Staff Director, National Commission for the Review of the National Reconnaissance Office

September 20, 2000

Mr. Kevin M. O'Connell	Executive Secretary, National Imagery and Mapping Agency Commission
Lt Gen Michael V. Hayden, USAF	Director, National Security Agency
Mr. Robert R. Soule	Director, Program Analysis & Evaluation, Office of the Secretary of Defense
LTG Edward G. Anderson, III, U.S. Army	Director for Strategic Plans & Policy (J-5), the Joint Staff
LTG James C. King, U.S. Army	Director, National Imagery and Mapping Agency

September 27, 2000

Mr. Larry Kindsvater	Executive Director, Intelligence Community Affairs, Office of the Director of Central Intelligence
Mr. James M. Simon, Jr.	Assistant Director of Central Intelligence for Administration
Gen Larry D. Welch, USAF (Ret.)	President, Institute for Defense Analysis and former Chief of Staff of the Air Force
Mr. Lawrence K. Gershwin	National Intelligence Officer for Science and Technology, National Intelligence Council

September 28, 2000

Ms. Cheryl Roby	Deputy Assistant Secretary of Defense for Programs and Evaluation, Office of the Assistant Secretary of Defense for Command, Control, Communications and Intelligence
The Honorable William S. Cohen	Secretary of Defense
The Honorable Rudy de Leon	Deputy Secretary of Defense
Gen Richard B. Myers, USAF	Vice Chairman, Joint Chiefs of Staff
The Honorable Joan A. Dempsey	Deputy Director of Central Intelligence for Community Management

October 11, 2000

Mr. Albert E. Smith	Executive Vice President, Lockheed Martin Space Systems Company
Mr. James W. Evatt	Executive Vice President, Boeing Space and Communications Group and President, Government Systems
Mr. Tig H. Krekel	President and Chief Executive Officer, Hughes Space and Communications Company
Mr. Timothy W. Hannemann	Executive Vice President and General Manager, TRW Space and Electronics Group

October 12, 2000

The Honorable R. James Woolsey	Partner, Shea & Gardner and former Director of Central Intelligence
RADM J. J. Quinn, USN	Commander, Naval Space Command
The Honorable James R. Schlesinger	Senior Advisor, Lehman Brothers and former Secretary of Defense, former Secretary of Energy, former Director of Central Intelligence

October 17, 2000 *Buckley Air Force Base, Denver, Colorado*

Lt Gen Roger G. DeKok, USAF	Vice Commander, Air Force Space Command

October 18, 2000 *Peterson Air Force Base, Colorado Springs, Colorado*

Lt Gen Roger G. DeKok, USAF	Vice Commander, Air Force Space Command
Lt Gen Eugene L. Tattini, USAF	Commander, Space and Missile Systems Center
Maj Gen Richard W. Davis, USAF	Director, National Security Space Architect, Office of the Assistant Secretary of Defense for Command, Control, Communications and Intelligence
Gen C. W. Fulford, Jr., USMC	Deputy Commander in Chief, U.S. European Command
COL (P) Richard V. Geraci, U.S. Army	Deputy Commanding General, Army Space, U.S. Army Space and Missile Defense Command
Maj Gen Thomas C. Waskow, USAF	Director of Air and Space Operations, Headquarters Pacific Air Forces
Lt Gen Maxwell C. Bailey, USAF	Commander, Air Force Special Operations Command
LTG Daniel G. Brown, U.S. Army	Deputy Commander in Chief, U.S. Transportation Command

RADM Martin J. Mayer, USN	Director for Strategy, Requirements and Integration (J-8), U.S. Joint Forces Command	
RADM Paul Sullivan, USN	Director for Plans (J-5), U.S Strategic Command	
MG Gary D. Speer, U.S. Army	Deputy Commander in Chief, U.S. Southern Command	

October 19, 2000 *Peterson Air Force Base, Colorado Springs, Colorado*

Maj Gen William R. Looney, III, USAF	Component Commander, U.S. Air Force Space Operations, U.S. Space Command
COL (P) Richard V. Geraci, U.S. Army	Deputy Commanding General, Army Space, U.S. Army Space and Missile Defense Command
CAPT Victor Cerne, USN	Joint Information Operations Center, U.S. Space Command
Col John T. Hill, USMC	Deputy, Naval Space Command
LTG Edward G. Anderson, III, U.S. Army	Deputy Commander in Chief and Chief of Staff, U.S. Space Command
Lt Gen George E.C. Macdonald, Canadian Forces	Deputy Commander in Chief, North American Aerospace Defense Command
Gen Ralph E. Eberhart, USAF	Commander in Chief, U.S. Space Command, Commander in Chief, North American Aerospace Defense Command and Commander, Air Force Space Command

October 25, 2000

Dr. David Whelan	Director, Tactical Technology Office, Defense Advanced Research Projects Agency
Lt Gen George K. Muellner, USAF (Ret.)	Vice President and General Manager-Phantom Works, The Boeing Company and former Principal Assistant to the Secretary of the Air Force for Acquisition
Mr. David A. Kier	Deputy Director, National Reconnaissance Office
Mr. Peter A. Marino	Chairman, National Imagery and Mapping Agency Commission

October 26, 2000

The Honorable Robert M. Gates	Interim Dean, George Bush School of Government and Public Service, Texas A&M University and former Director of Central Intelligence

October 31, 2000

Mr. Robert S. Zitz	Director, Initiatives Group, National Imagery and Mapping Agency
Mr. Fred Faithful	Director of Analysis and Plans, National Imagery and Mapping Agency
Mr. James M. Simon, Jr.	Assistant Director of Central Intelligence for Administration
Lt Gen Bruce Carlson, USAF	Director for Force Structure, Resources, and Assessment (J-8), the Joint Staff
Mr. David A. Kier	Deputy Director, National Reconnaissance Office
Dr. Lawrence J. Delaney	Assistant Secretary of the Air Force for Acquisition
Lt Gen Ronald T. Kadish, USAF	Director, Ballistic Missile Defense Organization

November 1, 2000

Mr. Andrew W. Marshall	Director, Net Assessment, Office of the Secretary of Defense
Dr. Taylor Lawrence	Vice President, Products and Technology, Northrop Grumman Corporation and former Staff Director, U.S. Senate Select Committee on Intelligence
Mr. David Thompson	President and Chief Executive Officer, Spectrum Astro
Gen Richard B. Myers, USAF	Vice Chairman, Joint Chiefs of Staff
Mr. John Copple	Chief Executive Officer, Space Imaging

November 14, 2000

VADM Lyle G. Bien, USN (Ret.)	Vice President, Government Programs, Teledesic LLC

November 15, 2000

Brig Gen Douglas J. Richardson, USAF	Commander, Space Warfare Center, Air Force Space Command, Schriever Air Force Base, Colorado

November 28, 2000

Commission Business

November 29, 2000

The Honorable Daniel S. Goldin	Administrator, National Aeronautics and Space Administration

November 30, 2000

    Commission Business

December 5, 2000

    The Honorable George J. Tenet   Director of Central Intelligence

December 12, 2000

    Commission Business

December 18, 2000

    Commission Business

December 19, 2000

    Commission Business

January 3, 2001

    Commission Business

January 4, 2001

    Commission Business

January 10, 2001

    Commission Business

January 11, 2001

    Deliver Report

Attachment D

Acknowledgements

The Commissioners wish to express their appreciation to the men and women of the U.S. Government national security space community who took time to discuss national security space organization and management with the Commissioners and the Commission Staff.

In particular, the Commissioners express their thanks to the Honorable Arthur L. Money, Assistant Secretary of Defense for Command, Control, Communications and Intelligence in the Office of the Secretary of Defense and the Honorable Keith Hall, Director of the National Reconnaissance Office.

Special thanks are extended to Major General H. J. "Mitch" Mitchell, USAF, the Department of Defense Liaison to the Commission. His knowledge of the current organization and management of national security space and his persistence in obtaining information for the Commission made its task much easier than it might have been.

The Commissioners would also like to thank the organizations that detailed personnel to staff the Commission: National Defense University, United States Air Force, U.S. Army Space and Missile Defense Command, Naval Research Laboratory, Federal Communications Commission, Goddard Space Flight Center and Central Intelligence Agency.

The National Reconnaissance Office and the Department of Defense's Washington Headquarters Services provided excellent administrative and logistical support under difficult time constraints. Thanks also are extended to the Central Intelligence Agency's Printing and Photography Group, which assisted in the design and publication of this report.

Attachment E

Glossary for Organization Charts

AF	Air Force
AFMC/CC	Commander, Air Force Materiel Command
AFRL	Air Force Research Laboratory
AFSPC/CC	Commander, Air Force Space Command
ASAF	Assistant Secretary of the Air Force
ASAF(A)	Assistant Secretary of the Air Force (Acquisition)
ASD (C3I)	Assistant Secretary of Defense (Command, Control, Communications, Intelligence)
C3	Command, Control, Communications
C3ISR	Command, Control, Communications, Intelligence Surveillance and Reconnaissance
CIA	Central Intelligence Agency
CINCNORAD	Commander in Chief, North American Aerospace Defense Command
CINCSPACE	Commander in Chief, United States Space Command
CIO	Chief Information Officer
CJCS	Chairman, Joint Chiefs of Staff
CMS	Community Management Staff
CSAF	Chief of Staff of the Air Force
DAC	Designated Acquisition Commander
DARPA	Defense Advanced Research Projects Agency
DCI	Director of Central Intelligence
DDCI/CM	Deputy Director of Central Intelligence/Community Management
DepSecDef	Deputy Secretary of Defense
DNRO	Director, National Reconnaissance Office
FBI	Federal Bureau of Investigation
J2	Directorate for Intelligence
NRO	National Reconnaissance Office
NSSA	National Security Space Architect
OSR	Office of Strategic Reconnaissance
PEO	Program Executive Officer
SAF/US	Under Secretary of the Air Force
SecAF	Secretary of the Army
SecArmy	Secretary of the Army
SecDef	Secretary of Defense
SecNav	Secretary of Navy
SMC/CC	Commander, Space and Missile Systems Center
USD	Under Secretary of Defense

www.ingramcontent.com/pod-product-compliance
Lightning Source LLC
Chambersburg PA
CBHW080735230426
43665CB00020B/2746